AMAZED AND AFRAID

DISCOVER THE POWER OF JESUS

A Catholic Guide for Small Groups

Copyright © 2017 by The Evangelical Catholic
All rights reserved.

Published by The Evangelical Catholic
6602 Normandy Lane FL 2
Madison, WI 53719
www.evangelicalcatholic.org

27 26 25 24 23 2 3 4 5 6

Nihil obstat: The Reverend Monsignor Michael Morgan, J.D., J.C.L.
Censor Librorum
September 5, 2023

Imprimatur: + Most Reverend Erik T. Pohlmeier
Bishop of St. Augustine
September 5, 2023

ISBN: 978-1-7371191-8-0
eISBN: 979-8-9891366-0-5

Scripture texts are taken from the Catholic Edition of the Revised Standard Version Bible, © 1965, 1966 by the Division of Christian Education of the National Council of the Churches of Christ in the United States of America. Used with permission. All rights reserved.

Excerpts from the English translation of the *Catechism of the Catholic Church* for use in the United States of America ©1994, United States Catholic Conference, Inc.—Libreria Editrice Vaticana.

Cover design by Andrea Jackson

No part of this publication may be reproduced, stored in a retrieval system, or transmitted in any form or by any means—electronic, mechanical, photocopy, recording, or any other—except for brief quotations in printed reviews, without the prior permission of The Evangelical Catholic.

Library of Congress Control Number: 2017941832

Contents

Introduction / 4

How to Use This Small Group Guide / 6

Week 1: Healing of the Paralytic / 10

Week 2: The Call of Matthew / 22

Week 3: Martha and Mary / 34

Week 4: Jesus Calls the First Disciples / 48

Week 5: Asleep in the Boat / 62

Week 6: The Way to the Father / 82

Appendices for Participants / 97

    A. Small Group Discussion Guide / 98

    B. A Guide to Seeking God / 101

    C. A Guide to the Sacrament of Reconciliation / 108

Appendices for Facilitators / 113

    D. The Role of a Facilitator / 114

    E. A Guide for Each Session of *Amazed and Afraid* / 120

    F. Leading Prayer and "Encountering Christ this Week" / 133

Small Group Discussion Guides from the Evangelical Catholic / 139

Introduction

People had strong reactions to Jesus of Nazareth as he traveled around Roman-occupied Israel preaching good news: "The kingdom of God is *really* close!" They either loved him or hated him so much that they wanted him dead.

What he did angered and frustrated people, even his friends. In every short account in this book, someone feels offended by the itinerant preacher from Galilee.

Lawyers were indignant: "Who do you think you *are*?"

"Religious" people were scandalized: "Why is your rabbi doing what *is not allowed!*"

His followers were beside themselves because he slept when they wanted him to rescue them: "Don't you *care?!*"

His friend resented him because she wanted him to be all about tasks, like she was, when he was about something else entirely: "Tell her to help me!"

Fishermen felt discounted because he asked them to push out to sea again when they knew the fish weren't biting: "Okay, we've *already* been out all night, but whatever."

His friends were frustrated and baffled when crisis was bearing down on them, and he said: "Don't be troubled." "But we don't know where you're going," they said. "How can we know *the way*?"

Everywhere you look in the New Testament, someone is asking, "Who *is* this guy, and why is he doing *that*?" A colorful group of characters followed him to find out: Roman collaborators who extorted money from other Jews to fatten their own wallets; fishermen who left behind their nets to become "fishers of men"; and women of all kind—married, and single women and even prostitutes. The answer they found so engaged them that they left everything behind to follow him.

For the last two millennia, a lot of people have asked the question "Who is this guy?" Many now prefer to ignore the carpenter from Nazareth who changed the world, but that doesn't make him any less commanding, his ways any less confrontational, his life any less compelling, or his invitation any less insistent than it has always been.

> "I stand at the door and knock; if any one hears my voice and opens the door, I will come in to him and eat with him [or her], and he [or she] with me."
> —Jesus, Revelation 3:20

Don't accept anyone else's ideas about who Jesus is. The stories and questions in this book will help you get to know Jesus yourself, either on your own or with a small discussion group. You'll see what he did, hear what he said, and meet the riveting characters who chose to follow him. Whether you're someone who has never met Jesus before in any meaningful way or someone who attends church regularly, reading and discussing these stories of Jesus and his followers will help you make your own decision about who he is and what that means for you.

Jesus may frustrate you too by what he says and does or by not doing what you want. Or he may engage your heart as he did the tax collectors, prostitutes, and fishermen. No matter what happens, however, you will come to understand why he has perturbed or engaged so many for so long.

Take the risk. Read the stories, ponder the questions with a small group or on your own, and try the spiritual exercises that accompany each story. Open the door, see who is there, and dine with him. You may find a feast beyond words.

The Evangelical Catholic

How to Use This Small Group Guide

Welcome to *Amazed and Afraid*, a small group guide to help people get to know Jesus of Nazareth, and help those who already know Jesus to encounter him more deeply.

Weekly Sessions

The weekly session material includes opening and closing prayer suggestions; the Scripture passages to be discussed that week; questions to prompt discussion, ideas or action; and suggestions to help you continue encountering Jesus through the week.

Unlike some small group Scripture discussion guides that progress consecutively through a book of the Bible, each session in this guide is self-contained. That way, if you or a friend attends a small group for the first time on Week 3, there won't be a need to "catch up." Anyone can just dive right in with the rest of the group. Instead of building sequentially, the sessions deepen thematically, helping you engage more with Jesus little by little.

The more you take notes, jot down ideas or questions, underline verses in your Bible (if you bring one to your small group, which we recommend!), and refer back to the previous sessions, the more God has the opportunity to speak to you through the discussion and the ideas he places in your heart. As with anything, the more you put in, the more you get back.

The best way to take advantage of each week's discussion is to carry the theme into your life by following the suggestions in the "Encountering Christ This Week" sections. Your small group facilitator will talk about the recommendations during each session. You will have a chance to ask questions and share experiences from previous weeks.

If you're not in a small group, *Amazed and Afraid* can help you come to know Jesus on your own. Consider the questions asked of each Scripture passage and follow up with the suggestions in "Encountering Christ This Week."

Appendices

Helpful appendices for both participants and facilitators supplement the weekly materials. Appendices A through C are for participants, and Appendices D through F are for group facilitators.

Prior to your first group meeting, please read Appendix A, "Small Group Discussion Guide." These guidelines will help every person in the group set a respectful tone that creates the space for encountering Christ together. This small group will differ from other discussion groups you may have experienced. Is it a lecture? No. A book club? No. Appendix A will help you understand what this small group is and how you can help seek a "Spirit-led" discussion. Every member is responsible for the quality of the group dynamics. This appendix will help you fulfill your role of being a supportive and involved group member.

Appendix B is a resource to enhance and deepen your relationship with Jesus. It encourages you to take the 1% Challenge™: pray at least fifteen minutes each day. That may sound like a lot, but this appendix also provides a step-by-step guide on how to spend the time.

In Appendix C, you will find a guide to the Sacrament of Reconciliation, commonly known as Confession. This sacrament bridges the distance we might feel from God that results from a variety of causes, including unrepented sin. If you want to grow closer to Jesus and experience great peace, the Sacrament of Reconciliation provides a fast track. This appendix will help alleviate any anxiety by leading you through the steps of preparing for and going to Confession.

While Appendices A through C are for small group participants and facilitators alike, Appendices D through F assist the facilitator in their role. A facilitator is not a teacher. His or her role is to buoy the conversation, encourage fruitful group discussion, and tend to the group dynamics.

Appendix D provides guidance and best practices for facilitating a small group successfully and includes recommendations for any difficult group dynamics that could arise. You will find guidelines on what makes a group work: building genuine friendships, calling for the Holy Spirit to be the group's true facilitator, and seeking joy together.

Appendix E takes the facilitator from the general to the specific, providing detailed leader notes for each session of *Amazed and Afraid*. Read these notes four or five days before each group meeting. They will help you prepare for each session by providing a heads-up on the content and issues that pertain to discussing particular Scripture passages.

Facilitators should read Appendix F well in advance of the first meeting. It has the guidance you need to lead prayer and encourage prayer by group members. While the material in each session includes a suggested prayer, this is only support material. It's far better spiritually for the group to pray in their own words. Appendix F guides the facilitator on how to help that happen.

Learning this skill is important. It will model for the group members how to talk to Jesus in their own words. Closing with extemporaneous prayer seals the time you have spent together by offering up the discoveries, questions, and joys of your conversation. Appendix F will help you guide your group from awkward beginnings to a deepening experience of talking to God.

Appendix F will also help the facilitator bring the "Encountering Christ This Week" section into the weekly discussion. It provides concrete suggestions on how to encourage and support group members in their personal engagement with the topics discussed. The facilitator plays a key role in helping participants allow Jesus to become more and more the center of their lives.

Enjoy the adventure!

week 1
Healing of the Paralytic

"My son, your sins are forgiven."
— Mark 2:5

Opening Prayer
Week One

Praying together in your own words is always more natural than reading a prayer together. Something simple and brief would be fine. You can ask the Lord's blessing on your time together or ask the Holy Spirit to guide your conversation, or you can just thank God for gathering you together to discuss the Scriptures. Begin and end the prayer with the Sign of the Cross, and you're ready to begin!

If extemporaneous prayer feels too difficult, one person should slowly read the following prayer aloud and invite the others to pray along silently in their hearts.

Week 1 | Healing of the Paralytic

All | In the name of the Father, and of the Son, and of the Holy Spirit. **Amen.**

Reader | Jesus, draw us close to you today. Open our hearts to hear what you have to say to us in this reading and discussion. Help us to trust you more. In your name we pray.

All | **Amen.**

Opening Discussion
Week One

Call to mind a time you had to overcome something difficult. What was the difficulty and what empowered you to overcome it?

Ask one person to read the Scripture passage aloud.

Mark

2:1-12

¹ And when he returned to Capernaum after some days, it was reported that he was at home. ² And many were gathered together, so that there was no longer room for them, not even about the door; and he was preaching the word to them. ³ And they came, bringing to him a paralytic carried by four men. ⁴ And when they could not get near him because of the crowd, they removed the roof above him; and when they had made an opening, they let down the pallet on which the paralytic lay. ⁵ And when Jesus saw their faith, he said to the paralytic, "My son, your sins are forgiven." ⁶ Now some of the scribes were sitting there, questioning in their hearts, ⁷ "Why does this man speak thus? It is blasphemy! Who can forgive sins but God alone?" ⁸ And immediately Jesus, perceiving in his spirit that they thus questioned within themselves, said to them, "Why do you question thus in your hearts? ⁹ Which is easier, to say to the paralytic, 'Your sins are forgiven,' or to say, 'Rise, take up your pallet and walk'? ¹⁰ But that you may know that the Son of man has authority on earth to forgive sins"—he said to the paralytic—¹¹ "I say to you, rise, take up your pallet and go home." ¹² And he rose, and immediately took up the pallet and went out before them all; so that they were all amazed and glorified God, saying, "We never saw anything like this!"

Encountering Christ in the Word
Week One

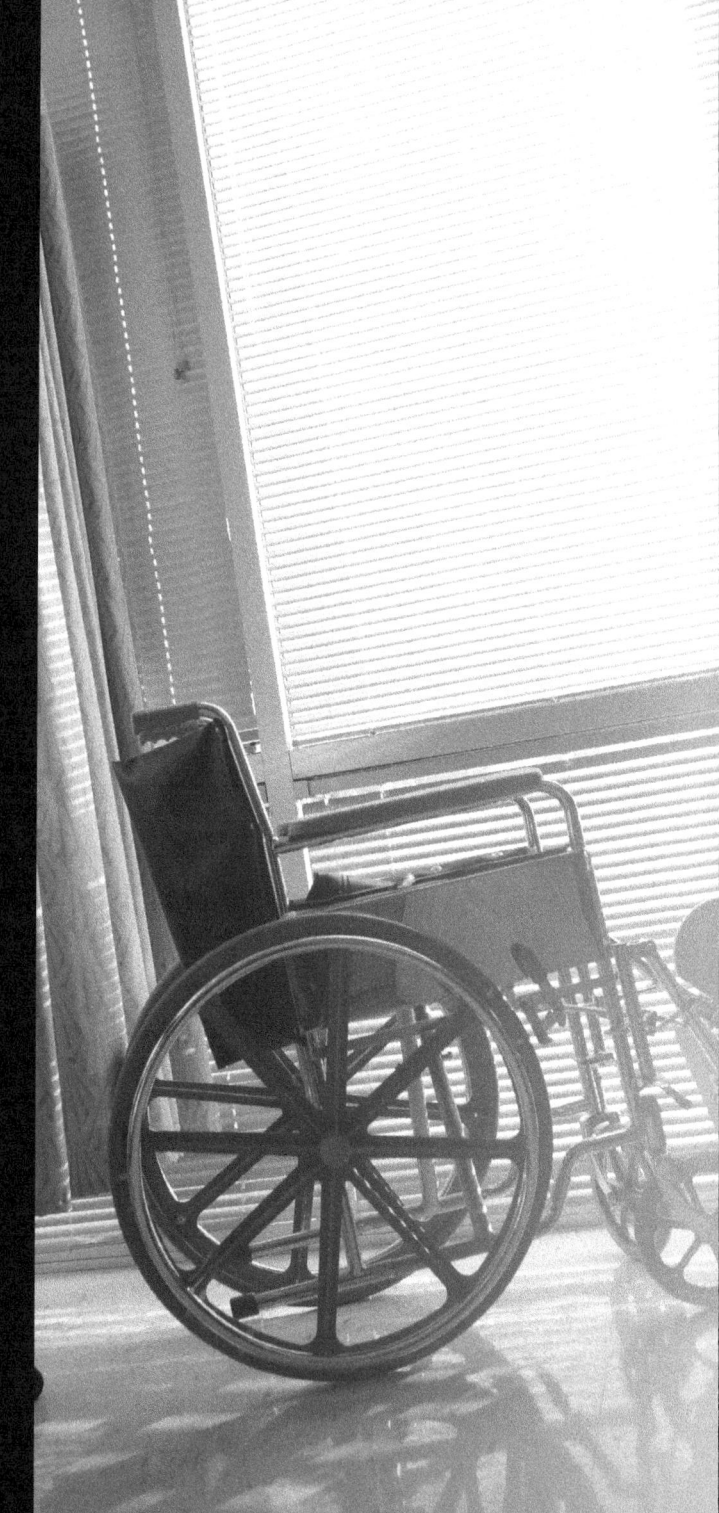

Week 1 | Healing of the Paralytic

1. What is the situation when this miracle takes place? Would someone summarize the scene in verses 1 and 2?

2. Take a moment to imagine what it would have required for the friends of the paralytic to get him to Jesus. *Pause.* Let's throw out ideas. Who would be willing to start?

3. How do you think the owner of the house and the crowd might have felt about all they saw the paralytic's friends do? What is the range of possibilities?

4. What is the first thing Jesus does when the man is lowered, and what does it say about his priorities?

5. How would you describe the scribes' reaction in verses 6-7?

6. What do you think Jesus wants the scribes to understand from his response to their questioning? (See the last part of verses 8-11.)

7. The last portion of verse 12 says, "They were all amazed and glorified God, saying, 'We never saw anything like this!'" The last word, "this," is ambiguous. To what could it refer?

8. The paralytic cannot reach Jesus by himself. Have you ever felt that there is a distance or an obstacle between you and God, and if so, what did you do about it?

9. Have friends or family ever taken you closer to Jesus? Would someone be willing to share about that?

10. The scribes didn't trust Jesus. His words in verse 5 raised questions "in their hearts" (verse 6). Does anything Jesus ever says or does raise questions in your heart?

11. How or where do you seek answers to these questions?

Encountering Christ This Week
Week One

You may wish to keep a journal during the six weeks of your small group or as you read this book on your own. Writing even in a simple spiral binder will help you collect and remember what God does in your heart.

Take time by yourself this week to read through the following Scripture passages, or others that attract you. Start with fifteen minutes on three days this week. If that is too much, try for ten and work up, or five and work up. What is important is that you begin!

Find a place where you won't be interrupted, somewhere you can close the door and avoid interruptions. First, ask the Holy Spirit to guide your reading, to help you hear what God wants to say to you through this Scripture verse or passage. After you've quieted your mind, read the passage and reflect on the following questions:

Day 1
Psalm 9:10
Romans 15:13

- What would it take for me to trust Jesus more?

Day 2
Mark 9:14-27

- Make a list of the things that distance you or put obstacles between you and God. In your prayer, imagine yourself handing over those things to Jesus.

Day 3
Isaiah 41:10
John 10:10

- Jesus healed the paralytic. What area of your life needs healing?

Closing Prayer
Week One

Have one person pray aloud while the others pray along silently.

All | In the name of the Father, and of the Son, and of the Holy Spirit. **Amen.**

Reader | Jesus, you are the great healer. We offer to you our doubts and questions that keep us from trusting you. Thank you for bringing us together in this group so that, like the paralytic's friends, we can bring one another closer to you. Help us to remain near you. In your name we pray.

All | **Amen.**

week **2**

The Call of Matthew

"'I desire mercy, and not sacrifice.' For I came not to call the righteous, but sinners."
— Matthew 9:13

Opening Prayer
Week Two

Have one person read the selection from Psalm 34 aloud. Have another person read aloud the prayer that follows while the others pray along silently.

All | In the name of the Father, and of the Son, and of the Holy Spirit. **Amen.**

Reader 1 | A reading from Psalm 34, verses 4-8 (NRSV):

⁴ I sought the Lord, and he answered me,
  and delivered me from all my fears.
⁵ Look to him, and be radiant;
  so your faces shall never be ashamed.
⁶ This poor soul cried out, and was heard by the Lord,
  and was saved from every trouble.
⁷ The angel of the Lord encamps
  around those who fear him, and delivers them.
⁸ O taste and see that the Lord is good;
  happy are those who take refuge in him.

All | **Amen.**

Reader 2 | Jesus, you take away our shame, and you make our faces radiant because you are the source of joy. Show us your mercy, and help us to experience your joy as we hear your word. Send your Holy Spirit to guide our discussion. Allow us to taste and see your goodness. Bless us in our time together as we pray, in the name of the Father, and of the Son, and of the Holy Spirit.

All | **Amen.**

Opening Discussion
Week Two

Think about what the word "mercy" means. **Pause.** Can someone give an example of a time when you or someone else showed mercy to another person?

Ask one person to read the Scripture passage aloud.

Matthew

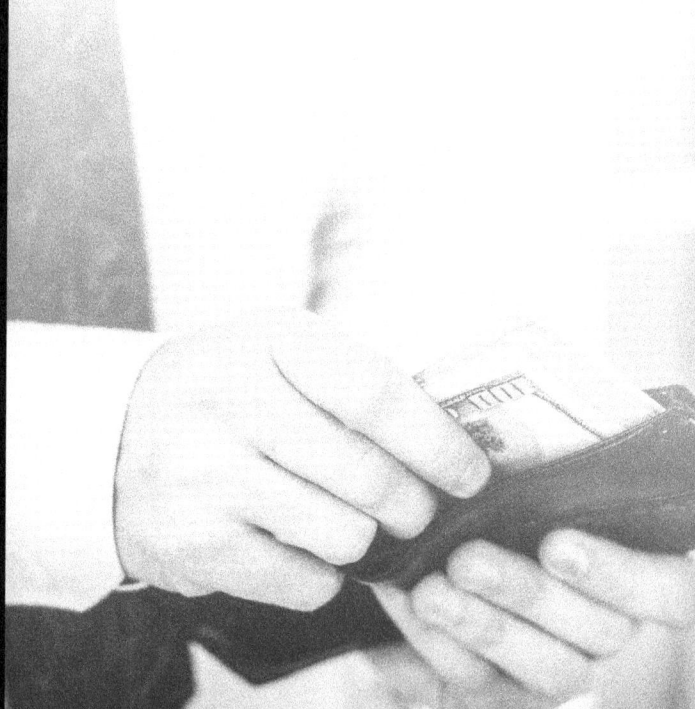

Week 2 | The Call of Matthew

⁹ As Jesus passed on from there, he saw a man called Matthew sitting at the tax office; and he said to him, "Follow me." And he rose and followed him.

¹⁰ And as he sat at table in the house, behold, many tax collectors and sinners came and sat down with Jesus and his disciples. ¹¹ And when the Pharisees saw this, they said to his disciples,

9:9-13

"Why does your teacher eat with tax collectors and sinners?" ¹² But when he heard it, he said, "Those who are well have no need of a physician, but those who are sick. ¹³ Go and learn what this means, 'I desire mercy, and not sacrifice.' For I came not to call the righteous, but sinners."

Encountering Christ in the Word
Week Two

Week 2 | The Call of Matthew

1. Tax collectors cheated people out of money they desperately needed. Why is this significant for this story?

2. In verse 9, Jesus asks Matthew to follow him while he is at work. What would be the immediate implications of leaving his post in the middle of the day?

3. What do you think Matthew might have felt when Jesus asked him to follow him?

4. Where does Jesus lead Matthew once they leave the tax office, and what could that indicate about Jesus' purposes?

5. What do you think Matthew felt when other tax collectors joined them at the table? How do you think these tax collectors and sinners found their way to this meal?

6. What do the Pharisees think of this situation? Try to make an argument from their perspective. What might be their reasoning?

7. Would anyone be willing to share about a time they felt like the Pharisees in this passage?

8. Read verse 12 again. What does Jesus mean by this analogy?

9. What do you think Jesus means in verse 13?

10. What do you think Matthew and the other tax collectors and sinners felt when Jesus made this statement about what the Pharisees needed to learn?

11. Would anyone be willing to share about how this passage speaks to you personally?

Encountering Christ This Week
Week Two

In Matthew 9:13, Jesus states, "Go and learn what this means, 'I desire mercy, and not sacrifice.'" The Latin word for mercy is *misericordia*. It contains within it the Latin word for heart: *cor*. Mercy for those who suffer comes from a movement of profound compassion in the heart. In the story of the calling of Matthew, we see Jesus' care and concern—the movement in his heart—for the tax collectors and sinners who were deemed unclean by the Pharisees and loathed by their countrymen.

This week spend at least fifteen minutes in prayer on four days. Suggestions for how to use that time appear on the following page. Or simply talk to God from your heart.

Each day, first ask the Holy Spirit to guide your reading, to help you hear what God wants to say to you through this Scripture verse or passage. After you've quieted your mind, read the passage and reflect on the questions. At the end, thank God for anything you felt or any inspirations that came to you during your prayer.

Day 1
Reread the story of Jesus calling Matthew. He saw something different in Matthew than what everyone else saw. Ask Jesus how he sees you. As you talk to Jesus, try to take your own good and righteous acts out of the picture if they come to mind. Ask Jesus about who you are to him, not about what you do.

Day 2
Read all of Psalm 32 and talk to God about any verses that stand out.

Day 3
During prayer, write down the ways you have experienced Jesus' blessings and anything you think he may be calling you to leave behind to follow him.

Day 4
Ask Jesus:
- How do you want me to follow you today?
- What in my heart do you want me to give to you?

If you want to reflect on other stories of Jesus' mercy, you could read the following Scripture passages. Read and pray with only one per day. Chew on it, seeking to understand what the Scripture really says or describes, and then ask, "What does this mean for me, Jesus?"

John 4:1-26
Luke 15:11-32
Ephesians 2:4-10
Philippians 2:1-11
Hebrews 12:1-4

Closing Prayer
Week Two

Have one person read the prayer aloud while the others pray along silently.

All | In the name of the Father, and of the Son, and of the Holy Spirit. **Amen.**

Week 2 | The Call of Matthew

Reader | Jesus, we thank you for gathering us together to discover more of your love and mercy. Open our hearts to the love and mercy your compassionate heart longs to show us. Help us to care more for those around us, as you have cared for us. We ask these things in your name.

All | **Amen.**

week 3
Martha and Mary

"You are anxious and troubled about many things."

— Luke 10:41

Opening Prayer
Week Three

Have one person read the selection from Psalm 46 aloud (verses 1, 7, 10-11). Have another person read aloud the prayer that follows while the others pray along silently.

All | In the name of the Father, and of the Son, and of the Holy Spirit. **Amen.**

Reader 1 | A Reading from Psalm 46

God is our refuge and strength,
 a very present help in trouble.

All | The Lord of hosts is with us;
 the God of Jacob is our refuge.

Reader 1 | "Be still, and know that I am God.
 I am exalted among the nations,
 I am exalted in the earth!"

All | The Lord of hosts is with us;
 the God of Jacob is our refuge.

Reader 2 | Lord of Hosts, be our refuge and strength today. Help us to encounter you together in your word and in one another. Thank you for your promise to be present as we gather in your name. Bless our conversation and prayer, in the name of the Father, and of the Son, and of the Holy Spirit.

All | **Amen.**

Opening Discussion
Week Three

Do you feel that you have balance in your life between busy activity and times of prayerful reflection? If not, what prevents making time for quiet in your life?

Ask one person to read the Scripture passage aloud.

Luke

⁳⁸ Now as they went on their way, he entered a village; and a woman named Martha received him into her house. ³⁹ And she had a sister called Mary, who sat at the Lord's feet and listened to his teaching. ⁴⁰ But Martha was distracted with much serving; and she went to him and said, "Lord, do you not care that my sister has left me to serve alone? Tell her then to help me."

10:38-42

⁴¹ But the Lord answered her, "Martha, Martha, you are anxious and troubled about many things; ⁴² one thing is needful. Mary has chosen the good portion, which shall not be taken away from her."

Encountering Christ in the Word
Week Three

Week 3 | Martha and Mary

1. What do we learn about Martha in this story? What qualities does this passage reveal? What might be some of her struggles in life?

2. Would someone be willing to share about what causes you to be anxious or troubled?

3. How does Jesus respond to Martha's request in verse 41, and what tone do you imagine he used? What do you think of his response?

4. What do we learn about Mary in this story? What qualities does she have? What might be some of her struggles in life?

5. On the whole, which of the two characters—Mary or Martha—do you relate to most, and why?

6. What do you do to be hospitable when someone visits your home? What does hospitality require from you personally?

7. Does this reflection on hospitality add anything to your understanding of this story?

8. In what ways do you experience the "good portion" (verse 42) of sitting at the feet of Jesus and listening to him? How could you seek more of this in your life?

9. Have you ever experienced the Lord changing your perspective (verse 42) after you have complained or asked for something, as Martha did? Would someone be willing to share about that?

10. How would you summarize the lessons in this story? What do you learn from it personally?

Next week the opening discussion focuses on the group's experiences with the following questions and prayers. Try to pray on Days 1 and 2, as well as on two additional days, so that you have something to share.

Luke 10:38 says that Martha "received [Jesus] into her house." The image of a house is often used in Scripture as a metaphor for the soul. "Behold, I stand at the door and knock," says Jesus in Revelation 3:20. "If any one hears my voice and opens the door, I will come in to him and eat with him, and he with me." Similarly, the Church adapts for use as the pre-Communion Mass prayer the Scripture verse in Matthew 8:8 of the centurion requesting Jesus to cure his servant without visiting his home: "Lord, I am not worthy that you should enter under my roof, but only say the word and my soul shall be healed."[1]

Early in the week, reflect prayerfully on the following questions. As in previous weeks, first ask the Holy Spirit to guide your thoughts and conversations, and afterward thank God for any inspirations or emotions you received.

---

[1] *The Roman Missal*, English Translation, 3rd Edition, 753.

Week 3 | Martha and Mary

Day 1

To what extent have you consciously welcomed Jesus into your "house"? Reflect on both your experiences and your desires.

- Was there a time in your life when you remember inviting Jesus into your heart for the first time, or was it more of a gradual invitation?
- If it was gradual, what do you remember as a possible starting point and/or key signs along the way?
- Perhaps your relationship with Jesus is something you have not ever really considered. If so, do you desire a relationship with Jesus?
- What would it take for you to want to invite Jesus into your heart?
- Is there anything that stands in the way?
- Talk to Jesus about any obstacles you identify.
- If you find you desire more of a relationship with Jesus, commit to scheduling time to talk to your small group leader or any other Christian whose faith you admire.
- If you're more comfortable talking to a pastoral professional, any priest or church pastoral staff person would love to have this conversation with you.
- No matter what, don't just leave that desire hanging unattended. Continue to talk to Jesus if you feel you're not ready to talk to someone else.

Day 2

- Martha is described as "distracted," "anxious" and "troubled" about "many things." What are some of the "many things" in your life that make you distracted or anxious?

- Martha clearly felt comfortable complaining to Jesus. Their relationship allowed her to be honest about how she felt.
- Do you take your complaints to God, or do you hold them in your heart against him, or against others?
- Take them to Jesus now and ask him to tend to them.
- Revisit in prayer the story of Martha and Mary after identifying your personal list of the "many things" (Luke 10:41). Before you read it, invite the Holy Spirit to speak a fresh word to you through this story.
- Meditate on Psalm 37, a great one for letting go of anxiety and troubles.

Day 3 Forward

Jesus praises Mary's practice of sitting at his feet and listening to him as the "one thing [that] is needful" (verse 42). There are many ways to do this, including daily Mass, if you're able to attend. You can always turn to God at any time of the day or night by reading a passage from a Gospel or an epistle, thinking about it, and then talking to Jesus about what it says.

Try to prioritize some "good portion" (verse 42) time each day for the rest of this week to be like Mary. Strive for at least fifteen minutes each day to sit at Jesus' feet and listen to him. Use the following Scripture passages to help you, or if you have favorites that draw you, feel free to use those. The passages below expand on some themes of the Martha and Mary story: anxiety, work, and prayer. We include more than you can use in case some don't appeal to you. Choose *only one per day* for meditation.

Meditation is simply reading and considering a passage, talking to God about your thoughts and questions, and then quietly waiting for God to reply. That doesn't mean you'll hear audible words or even know if a thought you have comes from God. Thoughts from God often come more frequently, though, as you read Scripture and learn to recognize God's voice. Simply allow a few moments of quiet to dispose your mind and heart to receive what God wants you to have, be it a thought or a feeling. That might come during your quiet time, or it could come later in the day. God is not limited by our time slots!

Matthew 11:28-30
Matthew 6:5-6
Philippians 4:6-7
Colossians 3:12-17
1 Peter 5:7

Closing Prayer
Week Three

Have one person read the prayer aloud while the others pray along silently.

All | In the name of the Father, and of the Son, and of the Holy Spirit. **Amen.**

Week 3 | Martha and Mary

Reader | God, teach us to find our peace in you alone. May our distractions, worries, and troubles be invitations to seek you with our whole heart. Help us choose "the good portion"—to spend time at your feet and hear you speak your loving counsel. Thank you for your presence among us today and always.

All | **Amen.**

week 4

Jesus Calls the First Disciples

"Put out into the deep and let down your nets for a catch."
— Luke 5:4

Opening Prayer — Week Four

Have one person lead the group in a brief spontaneous prayer, asking for inspiration and guidance in the discussion. To conclude, the person praying should invite the group to pray together the Our Father or some other well-known prayer.

All | In the name of the Father, and of the Son, and of the Holy Spirit. **Amen.**

Week 4 | Jesus Calls the First Disciples

Leader | Pray simply, thanking God for gathering you together and asking the Holy Spirit to guide the discussion.

Lord Jesus, thank you for . . .
Please bless our discussion today/tonight . . .

All | Our Father . . .
Amen.

Opening Discussion
Week Four

What ways were you challenged or blessed by the "Encountering Christ" section last week?

Ask one person to read the Scripture passage aloud.

Luke

5:1-11

¹ While the people pressed upon him to hear the word of God, he was standing by the lake of Gennes´aret. ² And he saw two boats by the lake; but the fishermen had gone out of them and were washing their nets. ³ Getting into one of the boats, which was Simon's, he asked him to put out a little from the land. And he sat down and taught the people from the boat. ⁴ And when he had ceased speaking, he said to Simon, "Put out into the deep and let down your nets for a catch." ⁵ And Simon answered, "Master, we toiled all night and took nothing! But at your word I will let down the nets." ⁶ And when they had done this, they enclosed a great shoal of fish; and as their nets were breaking, ⁷ they beckoned to their partners in the other boat to come and help them. And they came and filled both the boats, so that they began to sink. ⁸ But when Simon Peter saw it, he fell down at Jesus' knees, saying, "Depart from me, for I am a sinful man, O Lord." ⁹ For he was astonished, and all that were with him, at the catch of fish which they had taken; ¹⁰ and so also were James and John, sons of Zeb´edee, who were partners with Simon. And Jesus said to Simon, "Do not be afraid; henceforth you will be catching men." ¹¹ And when they had brought their boats to land, they left everything and followed him.

Encountering Christ in the Word
Week Four

Week 4 | Jesus Calls the First Disciples

1. Would someone please describe the beginning scene in detail? Where are they, and what is that place like? Who is there, and what are they doing? What might have been the atmosphere in the various groups?

2. What images from this story catch your attention?

3. What did Jesus tell Simon to do after he was done teaching, and how did Simon respond?

4. How do you think Simon felt about Jesus' request?

5. What does Simon do after the large catch of fish, and why do you think he responds that way?

6. Has anyone ever felt unworthy of God's gifts or mercy? *Pause.* Would someone be willing to share about your experience?

7. How did Jesus respond to Simon's reaction to the great catch? What did Jesus say? What do you imagine he did?

8. How might Jesus be calling you to go out "into the deep"? Is there anything in your life that feels challenging, frightening, or a like waste of time but that you think God may want you to do anyway? *Pause.* Would anyone be willing to share?

9. The end of the passage says, "They left everything and followed him" (verse 11). What might you need to leave in order to follow Jesus? *Pause.* Would someone be willing to share about that?

10. Has Jesus ever asked something of you that seemed impossible at the time? What happened?

Encountering Christ This Week
Week Four

Imagine Jesus saying to you, "Put out into the deep." Where would you lower your nets? Into areas of your life that are unsettled in some way, perhaps filled with fear, darkness, or doubt? Or would you prefer to avoid dangerous waters, not pushing out at all but rather staying safely ashore on solid ground?

This week try to press into what "the deep" is for you now—those parts of your life where you need God's peace and healing touch. Seek what God wants to do in your life. Is he telling you to push out further, even if to you it seems useless or hopeless? Perhaps he is asking you to "let down your nets" because he wants to pour out his abundance and show you his love. Jesus came to be with us in the midst of all our struggles. He meets us where we're at, no matter where we are. Whatever your deep waters may be, he will be there with you.

When Peter "put out into the deep" and came up with such a huge catch of fish, he knew he was in the presence of the divine. It made him fall on his knees and confess his sinfulness to the Lord. Going into the deep may make you also want to fall on your knees before Jesus. If so, do it! That's almost certainly an impulse from the Holy Spirit. Just that act will draw you closer to God. If you're Catholic, take that impulse into Confession, where God can touch and heal your heart through his forgiveness in the sacrament. Nothing has the power to transform pain and shame into abundant life as Reconciliation.

If you're squirming right now, you're not alone. It's natural to feel embarrassed or uncomfortable about Confession. Sin isn't pretty. Something is wrong with us if we don't feel bad when we hurt others, and hurting ourselves packs its own lasting punch, whether we feel guilty or not. Other times we don't find that we've done anything wrong, but perhaps we have not done what God *wants* us to do.

In either case, when we're afraid of Confession, we try to forget and move on, but the effects of sin *don't*. They remain within, hurting us. That's why the Church understands Reconciliation as a healing sacrament. God made us to be in relationship with him and with one another. He wired us that way. Sin short-circuits the wires. God's grace of forgiveness through the Sacrament of Reconciliation powerfully repairs our spiritual lives.

You might think, "I don't need to talk to a priest. I talk to God about my sins." Pope Francis says that's like confessing through e-mail!

> Some say: "Ah, I confess to God." But it's like confessing by e-mail, no? God is far away, I say things, and there's no face-to-face, no eye-to-eye contact. Paul confesses his weakness to the brethren face-to-face.[1]

Jesus knew how important face-to-face encounter is for us. He gave the power of freeing people from sin to the apostles in the upper room: "Whatever you loose on earth shall be loosed in heaven" (Matthew 16:19). Going to Confession gives guaranteed access to that power!

---

[1] "Pope Francis: Confess Sins with Concreteness and Sincerity," accessed at http://www.news.va/en/news/pope-francis-confess-sins-with-concreteness-and-si.

Don't let fear and discomfort keep you from the healing and consolation God wants to give you in the sacrament. It is a source of joy to you *and* God! "Do not be afraid!" said Jesus (Luke 5:10). "There will be more joy in heaven over one sinner who repents than over ninety-nine righteous persons who need no repentance" (15:7). You feel good when you confess because you partake of that joy.

Appendix C in this book has a guide to the Sacrament of Reconciliation to help you feel at ease. If that isn't sufficient to relieve your fears, talk to someone you know who participates in the sacrament and ask them about their experiences of Reconciliation. Even better, ask if they would accompany you to church when you go to Confession.

If you're not Catholic, the priest is available for spiritual counseling to you as much as he is available to Catholics. It's very comforting to share the weight of our burdens with another, especially with clergy who are trained and experienced in helping us walk with the Lord.

Whether you are a believer, nonbeliever, Catholic, or other Christian, God loves you and wants you to be with him, no matter what. "A broken and contrite heart, O God, thou wilt not despise" (Psalm 51:17). Often it's when we're most hurting that we open up to the healing the Lord wants to pour into our hearts and to the relationship he is always offering us.

Prayer

This week, commit to praying fifteen minutes *every* day. That's a step up from what you've been doing, but it will be worth it. That fifteen short minutes is only 1% of your day. You can give God that time, and he will give you more than you could have ever imagined—that great "catch" from deep waters.

A Scripture passage is suggested for each day. Read it, think about it, talk to God about it, rest in God with it. Try it every day, and notice any impact it makes on your daily life.

- Each time you pray for fifteen minutes, begin with a prayer asking the Holy Spirit to lead you to deep waters where God can reveal his grace.

- End by thanking God for any inspiring ideas, feelings, and resolutions that you received in prayer. Ask for the grace to act on what you've received and to live your life in gratitude for his gifts.

Matthew 7:7-12
Psalm 51
John 21:15-19
Ephesians 1:3-10
Luke 6:27-32
Hebrews 4:15-16

Closing Prayer
Week Four

Have one person pray aloud in his or her own words while the others pray along silently. Or use the following prayer.

All | In the name of the Father, and of the Son, and of the Holy Spirit. **Amen.**

Reader | Thank you, God, for inspiring us through our discussion. Help us to respond to the ways you're moving our hearts and the ideas you're putting into our minds. If there is something you want us to do, help us to recognize it and do it. Give us the courage we need to put out into the deep waters of life, and please meet us there.

All | **Amen.**

week 5
Asleep in the Boat

"Why are you afraid?"
— Mark 4:40

Ask someone to open with a simple prayer in their own words, and close with the following prayer as others pray along silently.

All | In the name of the Father, and of the Son, and of the Holy Spirit. **Amen.**

Reader | Lord, we need to hear your voice commanding, "Peace! Be still!"

The noise and chaos of life trouble our minds, and our hearts are often filled with fear.

We want to believe that you are with us and that you care about us.

Help us grow in trust of you.

Draw us to your presence and your peace.

In your name we pray.

All | **Amen.**

Opening Discussion
Week Five

What was the most frightening weather you ever experienced? What happened?

Ask one person to read the Scripture passage aloud.

Mark

Week 5 | Asleep in the Boat

4:35-41

⁳⁵ On that day, when evening had come, he said to them, "Let us go across to the other side." ³⁶ And leaving the crowd, they took him with them, just as he was, in the boat. And other boats were with him. ³⁷ And a great storm of wind arose, and the waves beat into the boat, so that the boat was already filling. ³⁸ But he was in the stern, asleep on the cushion; and they woke him and said to him, "Teacher, do you not care if we perish?" ³⁹ And he awoke and rebuked the wind, and said to the sea, "Peace! Be still!" And the wind ceased, and there was a great calm. ⁴⁰ He said to them, "Why are you afraid? Have you no faith?" ⁴¹ And they were filled with awe, and said to one another, "Who then is this, that even wind and sea obey him?"

Encountering Christ in the Word
Week Five

Week 5 | Asleep in the Boat

1. Would someone please list in order the sequence of events in the story?
2. What do these details add to your understanding of the story?
3. What do you think Mark means when he says that the disciples "took [Jesus] with them, just as he was" (verse 36)? Why would he mention this?
4. In light of the rest of the story, how do you think Jesus "was" when they set sail?
5. Describe what it would have been like to be in the boat as the storm rose. Include how you think the disciples felt physically and emotionally.
6. How does Jesus respond to the disciples after quieting the storm, and how do you think they felt about this? What do you think about Jesus' reaction?
7. What could the disciples have done to show greater faith?
8. If you ever had a time of fear, frustration, or something else that caused you to try to "wake up Jesus," do you feel it was caused by lack of faith? Why or why not?
9. After Jesus calmed the storm, it says the disciples "were filled with awe." Have you ever felt awe? How would you describe it?
10. If you've had a time in your life when you felt that Jesus didn't care what was happening to you, how did you handle it?
11. How does this passage challenge you to handle times of uncertainty and fear in your life?
12. What will be difficult about this challenge? How can you grow into greater faith?

This week, again pray every day, but on three days try to expand the fifteen minutes you've been praying to thirty. Giving more time to God will dispose you to receive more of his grace!

Don't let the longer time period intimidate you. If it feels impossible, it's better to stay with fifteen minutes and pray regularly than to aim for something you can't achieve and possibly miss prayer altogether.

If you don't usually attend daily Mass, try it in conjunction with one of your prayer times this week. Think about praying the liturgy with your whole heart, with the kind of awe that the disciples felt when Jesus quieted the storm. You could spend fifteen minutes in private prayer before or after Mass that day.

Below you will find prayer prompts to help you fill thirty minutes easily on the days you pray longer. As always, begin by asking the Holy Spirit to guide your reading, thoughts, and conversation with God.

Day 1

The method of praying with Scripture described here is an ancient prayer of the Church called *lectio divina*. (Appendix B also describes this prayer method.) It is a timeless aid for seeking God through the Scriptures.

Week 5 | Asleep in the Boat

- Find a place where you won't be interrupted. Ask God to guide your prayer time. Reread Mark 4:35-41, either from this book or, even better, in your own Bible. Underline or make note of whatever stands out for you. Did you notice anything this time that you hadn't during your small group? That could be the Holy Spirit showing you something God wants you to see.

- If anything stood out in this reading, or if something seems to you to be missing from the story, spend time thinking about it. What might this mean for you, or how might it apply in your life? Do any feelings arise? Talk to the Holy Spirit about anything that comes to mind.

- Don't rush this meditation. Return to the text again, especially if questions come to mind. Sometimes even a mundane question such as "What did it say after that?" can be the Holy Spirit drawing your attention to where God wants it.

- After you have thought about this Scripture passage and talked to the Holy Spirit about it, ask God if he wants you to do anything. If something comes to mind, commit in your heart to when, where, and how you will do it. Make a note in a journal or planner so that you won't forget.

- Rest quietly with God to seal whatever you have received.

- As you close your prayer time, thank God for any insights you received or ways your heart was stirred.

Day 2

Imagine Yourself in the Boat during the Storm

St. Ignatius of Loyola, founder of the Jesuits, taught his followers and students to pray imaginatively. He believed our imaginations are *the* privileged place in the interior life because through them God can speak to us very directly.[1]

Reread Mark 4:35-41. Then take time to imagine the scene in detail, putting yourself into the story. This simple outline may be helpful, or return to the biblical text itself, or just use your imagination.

- Imagine you're one of the disciples standing near the Sea of Galilee as Jesus teaches the crowds. Draw on your memory of a real lake to hear the waves, smell the water, and feel the temperature of the air at the end of the day ("evening had come," verse 35). Spend several minutes in this "composition of place," as St. Ignatius called it. Note any details that come to mind, especially anything unusual or unexpected. God may be speaking to you through it.

- Fill in the scene. What do you see happening? Watch the people pushing forward to hear Jesus. What do you feel? Hear Jesus say to you directly, "Let's cross to the other side." What does this mean for you in particular? How does it make you feel? Be honest—negative responses are fine! God wants you as you are!

---

[1] Read more about this at ignatianspirituality.com in the Ignatian Prayer section; find online at http://www.ignatianspirituality.com/ignatian-prayer/the-spiritual-exercises/ignatian-prayer-and-the-imagination.

- Imagine hustling Jesus into a boat and then jumping in, pushing off from shore with the other disciples. See the other boats accompanying you and Jesus. What are your feelings, thoughts, or questions? Talk to Jesus about anything that comes to mind.
- Now what happens? Are you rowing, or are you doing something else? See the shore recede. Watch Jesus lie down at the back of the boat with the cushion. What do you think or feel?
- Feel the force of the wind picking up and the waves that "beat into the boat" (verse 37). See the water coming into the boat. Look at the faces of the disciples, some of them fishermen who grew up on the lake. What do you see in their eyes? What do they say?
- Turn to sleeping Jesus again. What do you feel? What do you do?
- If you haven't already, awaken Jesus. Ask him, "Don't you care about me?!"
- See Jesus stand and command the storm: "Peace! Be still!" (verse 39). What do you feel now?
- See Jesus looking into your eyes and asking, "Why are you so afraid?" Answer him. Tell him anything you think or feel.
- Now do whatever you want: sit back on the cushion with Jesus after the storm is quieted. Yell at him for being asleep when you were frightened and in danger. Throw yourself into his arms in tears. The possibilities are infinite. Trust God to prompt your heart.

Close the prayer by thanking God for any insights you have received. If you feel you didn't receive any, ask God to open your heart to whatever ways he is trying to speak to you.

A Second Alternative

If you're more visual than imaginative, use this Rembrandt painting of the storm for your meditation. You may feel that a single person in the boat represents you at this time in your life, or you may identify with several of them. Ask God to show you anything he wants you to see in any or all of the disciples.

Taking the Lead
The man in the bow of the ship is on top, riding the huge wave. He's a professional on the water. Is this the disciple you would be in the boat? Are you focused on work, earnestly trimming the front sail? Do you feel panicked, or is this more of an adventure? Do you feel exhausted thinking about it, or exhilarated?

Fixing the Problem
Three of the men (probably experienced sailors/fishermen also) are at the mast, working frantically trying to fix the main sail. The gale winds have ripped it and snapped the rope that attaches the boom to the mast. This would prevent them from steering the safest way into the waves. Is this you, someone who tries to solve the technical problems? Someone who feels they can't direct things where they desperately need to go? How do you feel as you work to reattach the boom?

Barely Hanging On
A huge wave is pounding the man on the left in the middle. He is hanging onto a rope, looking terrified. Is this you? Do you feel like you're barely hanging on in life as Jesus sleeps?

Afraid

Most of the crew seem afraid, but especially the man on the right side of the boat. He is crouched over and looking terrified at the enormous wave that is swamping the boat. Is this you, frozen by anxiety?

Sick

On the lower left in the back is a distressed man with his hand on his forehead, leaning over the side of the boat, perhaps about to throw up. Is this you? Are you physically debilitated by the storms of life?

Angry at God

Two disciples appear angry at Jesus for sleeping in the storm. One shakes him awake, and the other seems to be the one saying, "Teacher! Don't you care if we perish?" Is this you, shouting at Jesus, wanting to know why he isn't there for you in the difficulties of your life?

Quiet and Alone

On the lower left of the boat is a man in white, his back facing us. He sits still and alone, almost as though he is separated from the storm and the chaotic activity all around him. He seems to be looking at a shadowy figure. Is this you, escaping into your mind rather than facing life, or maybe finding consolation in your own dreams and visions? What else could the shadowy figure be for you?

Lost
A man stands behind the man in white on the left side of the boat, holding a rope. His other hand is on his forehead as he stares blankly out at the dark sea. Is this you, looking elsewhere, not at Jesus who is so close? What are you seeking? Why don't you look at Jesus?

One at Peace
Only the kneeling disciple at Jesus' feet looks at Jesus with trust and reverence. Rembrandt has even painted a halo on this disciple's head. Is this you? Do you look to Jesus and trust him, no matter what is happening all around? Do you feel blessed by his presence?

At the Helm
In the stern, at the very back, sits the disciple at the helm, holding the tiller. He must be another experienced fisherman. He is in charge of the boat, responsible for guiding its course and instructing the crew what they need to do. Is this you? Are you guiding a group through a storm? Ask God to speak whatever your heart wants to know, or to give you what you need.

Jesus
Complete your meditation by looking closely at Jesus. How has Rembrandt painted him? What do you feel toward this Jesus, at peace when his disciples are in such great danger?

Listen to God
After you've identified yourself in the boat, ask the Lord what word he has for you in the storm. Pray quietly about this to close your meditation.

Day 3

Meditate on this passage from the autobiography of St. Thérèse of Lisieux, *Story of a Soul*:

> I suffered complete spiritual dryness, almost as if I were quite forsaken. As usual, Jesus slept in my little boat. I know that other souls rarely let him sleep peacefully, and he is so wearied by the advances he is always making that he hastens to take advantage of the rest I offer him. It's likely that as

far as I'm concerned, he will stay asleep until the great final retreat of eternity. But that doesn't upset me. It fills me with great joy. . . . I should be distressed that I drop off to sleep during my prayers and during my thanksgiving after Holy Communion. But I don't feel at all distressed. I know that children are just as dear to their parents whether they are asleep or awake and I know that doctors put their patients to sleep before they operate. So I just think that God "knows our frame; he remembers that we are dust." [2]

[2] *Story of a Soul*, trans. John Beavers (Garden City: Doubleday/Image, 1957), 99–100.

Closing Prayer
Week Five

Have one person read the prayer aloud while the others pray along silently.

All | In the name of the Father, and of the Son, and of the Holy Spirit. **Amen.**

Week 5 | Asleep in the Boat

Reader | Father, I know what it is like to be
gripped with fear,
not just for a moment of time,
but for weeks on end.
This is no way for a Christian to live.
Thank you for strengthening my faith,
and the faith of my brothers and sisters.
Thank you for sending Jesus to rescue
and redeem us.
Thank you for sending the Holy Spirit to
dwell with us and in us.
Thank you that not a sparrow falls
to the ground
without you knowing it.
Thank you for the comfort of your presence.
Please forgive me for my unbelief.
Please teach me, and strengthen me
so that my faith will reflect your greatness.
Thank you for your great patience with me.
In Jesus' name, I pray.[1]

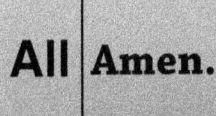

All | **Amen.**

---

[1] Adapted from http://www.jesuswalk.com/lessons/8_22-25.htm.

week **6**

The Way to the Father

"Let not your hearts be troubled."

— John 14:1

Opening Prayer
Week Six

Have someone open with a simple prayer in their own words. Close with the following prayer from Psalm 84 as others pray along silently.

All | In the name of the Father, and of the Son, and of the Holy Spirit. **Amen.**

Reader 1 How lovely is thy dwelling place,
  O L͟o͟r͟d͟ of hosts!
2 My soul longs, yea, faints
  for the courts of the L͟o͟r͟d͟;
my heart and flesh sing for joy
  to the living God.

3 Even the sparrow finds a home,
  and the swallow a nest for herself,
  where she may lay her young,
at thy altars, O L͟o͟r͟d͟ of hosts,
  my King and my God.
4 Blessed are those who dwell in
    thy house,
  ever singing thy praise! . . . .
10 For a day in thy courts is better
  than a thousand elsewhere.

All **Amen.**

Opening Discussion
Week Six

What was your experience with last week's "Encountering Christ" prayer exercises?

Imagine that you're leaving a job or a roommate situation, or anything that involves long-standing relationships and shared purpose. Ideally, it should be something real, from your past or present life.

What kind of instructions or parting words do you think you would want to say to those you're leaving behind? What is most important for them to know?

Ask one person to read the Scripture passage aloud.

John

Week 6 | The Way to the Father

¹"Let not your hearts be troubled; believe in God, believe also in me. ² In my Father's house are many rooms; if it were not so, would I have told you that I go to prepare a place for you? ³ And when I go and prepare a place for you, I will come again and will take you to myself, that where I am you may be also.

⁴ And you know the way where I am going." ⁵ Thomas said to him, "Lord, we do not know where you are going; how can we know the way?" ⁶ Jesus said to him, "I am the way, and the truth, and the life; no one comes to the Father, but by me. ⁷ If you had known me, you would have known my Father also; henceforth you know him and have seen him."

14:1-11

⁸ Philip said to him, "Lord, show us the Father, and we shall be satisfied." ⁹ Jesus said to him, "Have I been with you so long, and yet you do not know me, Philip? He who has seen me has seen the Father; how can you say, 'Show us the Father'? ¹⁰ Do you not believe that I am in the Father and the Father in me? The words that I say to you I do not speak on my own authority; but the Father who dwells in me does his works. ¹¹ Believe me that I am in the Father and the Father in me; or else believe me for the sake of the works themselves."

Encountering Christ in the Word
Week Six

Week 6 | The Way to the Father

1. What things does Jesus tell his disciples to do in this Scripture passage? Let's name and discuss them.

2. Which of these instructions stands out or means the most for you, and why?

3. Jesus says many things about himself in this passage. Let's take a few minutes to name and discuss them.

4. Now which of the things Jesus says about himself stands out the most to you, and why?

5. How do you respond to the idea that Jesus prepares a place for you in his Father's house, a place for you to be "with him"?

6. What do you imagine the Father's house to be like?

7. How do the disciples react to the many things Jesus says? Why do you think they reacted this way?

8. What do we know about God from this passage?

9. What do you think Jesus means by saying that he is "the way, and the truth, and and the life" (verse 6)?

10. Which of Jesus' parting instructions is the most important for your life right now?

Jesus says the disciples *know* the way to the Father's house because they have been with him all the time. But they are confused by what he says, as we often are, and their minds are troubled even though Jesus says they shouldn't be.

Our minds are often troubled too. Jesus' words on the night he was arrested indicate that even when circumstances are as bad as they can be, because we know him, we know God, and that changes everything. We can seek and find God's peace.

We hope that through the six weeks of this study, you've come to know Jesus better and that knowing him better makes you want to know him more! Some of the greatest minds and hearts in history, from St. Augustine to Mother Teresa, found Jesus captivating; knowing him transformed their lives.

You can have this too. Jesus wants every one of us to know him and love him so that we can flourish and help others flourish as well. "I came that they may have life, and have it abundantly" (John 10:10). "He who believes in me, as the scripture has said, 'Out of his heart shall flow rivers of living water'" (John 7:38).

Jesus is always reaching out to us, hoping we will seek him so that he can lead us to the Father's house. He doesn't stop because this small group ends or pauses for a time. As we said in Week 3, in the "Encountering Christ This Week" exercise, he is always trying to get to us: "Behold, I stand at the door and knock; if any one hears my voice and opens the door, I will come in to him and eat with him, and he with me" (Revelation 3:20).

Open the door. Open it every day of your life. That is how you will come to know Jesus better, especially when you meet him in the Scriptures. Seek him there with your whole heart and mind.

This week, set aside fifteen to thirty minutes each day to pray with the Scripture passages suggested on the next two pages, or another Scripture to which God leads you. Prayerfully read it several times. Talk to God about what stirs in your heart from each reading. If you have more time or don't know what to pray about, reflect on the text provided. Recall the discussion on John 14:1-11, and relate it to the Scripture passage you have just read. Honestly lift your deepest thoughts and feelings to God, and then be quiet so that you can listen.

In the future, when you don't have these prayer prompts, try reading through a book of the Bible. Start with a Gospel; Mark is the shortest and most straighforward. Work up to reading the epistles, the best guides out there for how to follow Jesus more closely. The EC recommends Ephesians, Philippians, 2 Corinthians, and James as great guides for growing as disciples. The daily readings of the liturgy provide rich food for meditation. They can be found easily by searching online for "Catholic daily Mass readings."

Always begin by quieting your mind and asking the Holy Spirit to guide your prayer. End by thanking God for any inspirations, feelings, or resolutions that came to mind. Make a note of them so you don't forget, particularly if you resolved to do something because of your conversation with Jesus.

"Ask, and it will be given you; seek, and you will find; knock, and it will be opened to you."
— Matthew 7:7

Day 1
Psalm 84:1-4, 10

Do I believe that a day living with God is better than a thousand elsewhere? Where would I rather be than with God?

Jesus, teach my heart to sing for joy at the thought of our Father's house. Increase my desire to be with you.

Day 2
1 John 3:1-3

Do I really believe I am a child of God? Although we don't yet know what eternity shall make us, do I hope to be like Jesus? Do I feel genuine anticipation to see him someday "as he is"?

Jesus, help me feel that your Father in heaven is my Father, your Mother, my Mother. I want to believe I am a child of God, and I look forward to the day I go home to God and see you as you really are.

Day 3
2 Corinthians 5:1-5

What is my vision of heaven like? How does that compare with the image of the Father's house?

Jesus, thanks to you, the end of my life on earth is not the end. This life is hard at times, and I groan and sigh with anxiety as I long for the glory of heaven to be my reality. Thank you for the promise of heaven.

Day 4
Ephesians 2:18-22

Do I feel more like a stranger or a citizen of the household of God? Why do I feel that way?

Father, you have adopted me (or want to adopt me)! I am no longer lost and orphaned. Bring me into your heavenly household. Help me feel honored to be invited into your household, not only in heaven, but on earth as well!

Day 5
John 15:7-9

What does it look like for me to abide in Jesus? How can I abide in his love more?

Jesus, lead me deeper into your love so that I may glorify you with a fruitful life of discipleship.

Day 6
John 15:15-16

Why did God choose me? What do I need to ask from God to be able to bear fruit for him?

Thank you, Jesus, for choosing me and calling me your friend. Help me to know what I need so that I can ask for that grace from you.

Day 7
1 Corinthians 12:4-7, 28

What gifts has God given me? What works am I called to do with them for the good of others?

Holy Spirit, help me receive the gifts God longs to give me. Open my heart to recognize and accept them.

Closing Prayer
Week Six

Take turns praying aloud in your own words. After you've voiced your own thanksgiving, petitions, and praises, have one person read the prayer aloud while the others pray along silently.

All | In the name of the Father, and of the Son, and of the Holy Spirit. **Amen.**

Reader | Jesus, thank you for being a true friend to us,
for showing us the way to the Father.
Father, thank you for inviting us to live with you
for eternity in your heavenly house.
Holy Spirit, thank you for inspiring us
to continue the good works of Jesus,
which are prepared for me to do on this earth.
Holy God, strengthen our faith,
and help us to believe in you more wholly.
Increase our desire for you,
so that we may choose to be with you always.
In Jesus' name, we pray.

All | **Amen.**

Appendices for Participants

A. Small Group Discussion Guide

B. A Guide to Seeking God

C. A Guide to the Sacrament of Reconciliation

Appendix

A small group seeks to foster an honest exploration of Jesus Christ with one another. For many, this will be a new experience. You may be wondering what will take place. Will I fit in? Will I even want to come back?

Here are some expectations and values to help participants understand how small groups work as well as what makes them work and what doesn't. When a group meets for the first time, the facilitator may want to read the following aloud and discuss it to be sure people understand small group parameters.

Purpose
We gather as searchers. Our express purpose for being here is to explore together what it means to live the gospel of Jesus Christ in and through the Church.

Priority
In order to reap the full fruit of this personal and communal journey, each one of us will make participation in the weekly gatherings a priority.

Participation
We will strive to create an environment in which all are encouraged to share at their comfort level.

We will begin and end all sessions in prayer, exploring different ways to pray together over time. We will discuss a Scripture passage at every meeting. Participants do not need to read the passage beforehand—no one needs to know anything about the Bible in order to participate. The point is to discuss the text and see how it applies to our own lives.

Discussion Guidelines

The purpose of our gathering time is to share in "Spirit-filled" discussion. This type of dialogue occurs when the presence of the Holy Spirit is welcomed and encouraged by the nature and tenor of the discussion. To help this happen, we will observe the following guidelines:

- Participants strive always to be respectful, humble, open, and honest in listening and sharing: they don't interrupt, respond abruptly, condemn what another says, or even judge in their hearts.

- Participants share at the level that is comfortable for them personally.

- Silence is a vital part of the experience. Participants are given time to reflect before discussion begins. Keep in mind that a period of comfortable silence often occurs between individuals speaking.

- Participants are enthusiastically encouraged to share while at the same time exercising care to permit others (especially the quieter members) an opportunity to speak. Each participant should aim to maintain a balance: participating without dominating the conversation.

- Participants keep confidential anything personal that may be shared in the group.

- Perhaps most important, participants should cultivate attentiveness to the Holy Spirit's desire to be present in the time spent together. When the conversation seems to need help, ask for the Holy Spirit's intercession silently in your heart. When someone is speaking of something painful or difficult, pray that the Holy Spirit comforts that person. Pray for the Spirit to aid the group in responding sensitively and lovingly. If someone isn't participating, praying for that person during silence may be more helpful than a direct question. These are but a few examples of the ways in which each person might personally invoke the Holy Spirit.

Time
We meet weekly because that is the best way to become comfortable together, but we can schedule our meetings around any breaks or holidays when many people will be away.

It is important that our group start and end on time. Generally a group meets for about ninety minutes, with an additional thirty minutes or so afterward for refreshments. Agree on these times as a group and work to honor them.

Appendix

The 1% Challenge™: Fifteen Minutes a Day with God's Word

> 1% of your day is fourteen minutes and
> twenty-four seconds.
> How you spend that time could change your life!

*Unless you are convinced that prayer is the best use of
your time, you will never find time to pray.*
—Fr. Hilary Ottensmeyer, OSB[1]

If only I had the time!

Time—we only have so much of it each day. All kinds of demands chip away the hours. Modern communication and social media increase our sense of urgency. No wonder we experience conflicting desires over how to spend our time.

One thing we all know for certain: relationships require time. Friendships don't form or last unless people spend time together. Marriages struggle when spouses don't make time to talk and listen deeply to one another. Parents who do not prioritize spending time with their children risk painfully regretting that decision down the road. Some things never change. We were made for relationships, and relationships take time.

---

[1] Accessed at http://www.saintmeinrad.edu/seminary-blog/echoes-from-the-bell-tower/posts/2015/monastic-time.

So how about our relationship with God?
Just as all relationships require time, so too does a deepening friendship with God. What kind of relationship do you have with the person in your neighborhood with whom you've never had a personal conversation? Even if you take out her garbage can weekly because she is disabled, she is an acquaintance, not a friend. Friends spend time together. Jesus called us his friends (John 15:15).

One way we spend time with Jesus is at Mass. This will always be the center, source, and summit of our prayer lives. But without personal time with Jesus outside liturgies, the encounter at Mass can resemble meeting that neighbor at a block party: talking for a few minutes without any deep connection. The mysterious reality of that person remains remote.

How much time should I spend in personal prayer?
A little goes a long way with God.

Take the 1% Challenge™: for thirty days, spend at least fifteen minutes a day with God and God's Word.

If you do, you'll never want to leave it behind.

We've seen it happen again and again. When people build a habit of talking and listening to God, they

- begin to know the Lord in ways that affect them personally;
- grow in their ability to hear God's voice and follow his gentle guidance;

- experience more of the Lord's love, peace, and joy—even in difficult circumstances;
- become more attentive to other people, because in prayer, Christ gives us his compassion for every person.

It is not easy, at least not at first. But prayer begets prayer. As you experience the fruit of a deeper friendship with the Lord, your desire for God grows. Your heart longs more and more to *build your life around prayer* rather than just *squeezing it in*. Hunger for God grows when you taste the sweetness of Jesus' company and experience the joy of a Christ-centered life.

How should I spend my fifteen minutes?

Always begin by recognizing that God is with you. He is with you even when you're not paying attention. When you attend to God, you are simply focusing on reality.

St. Teresa of Avila called prayer "an intimate sharing between friends."[2] Any good friendship involves three things: talking, listening, and simply being together.

1. Talk to God

There is no wrong way to talk to God. Talk about anything on your mind. Keep it real; don't just say what you think a prayerful person should say or what you think God wants to hear. Even saying, "Lord, help me to pray" is itself a prayer.

If you're stuck, keep in mind the first three things we all learn to say as children: *"Thank you," "I'm sorry,"* and *"Please."* That's a great outline for a chat with God—it's as simple as that!

---

[2] Teresa of Avila, *The Book of Her Life*, translated, with notes, by Kieran Kavanaugh, O.C.D. and Otilio Rodriguez, O.C.D (Indianapolis/Cambridge: Hacket Publishing Company, Inc., 2008), 44.

2. Listen to God
Morning after morning he opens my ear that I may hear" *(cf. Isaiah 50:4).*

No matter how impossible it may seem, you can learn to discern the Lord's voice in your life. It takes practice and guidance, but never forget the promise of Jesus: "My sheep hear my voice, and I know them, and they follow me" (John 10:27). Jesus means what he says—this is attainable!

The fastest way to learn to recognize the voice of God is to read the Scriptures prayerfully. The Bible truly is God's word expressed in human words. With the Holy Spirit coming to our aid, reading it becomes "a life-giving encounter" (Pope St. John Paul II, *Novo Millennio Ineunte*, 39). On the following pages, a simple outline of *lectio divina* will help you to find what the Lord wants to say to you through Scripture. *Lectio divina* is a time-tested way of encountering the voice of the living God in Scripture.

3. Be with God
Sometimes words get in the way of deeper communication. St. John of the Cross said, "The Father spoke one Word, which was his Son, and this Word he speaks always in eternal silence, and in silence must it be heard by the soul."[3] The Lord says, "Be still, and know that I am God" (Psalm 46:10).

Begin and end each prayer time with a minute or two of silence to rest in God's presence. You probably won't hear anything audible or even sense anything interiorly, but be confident that God is filling that silence in ways you cannot immediately perceive. Often something can become very clear later in the day after a time of silence in the morning.

---

[3] *The Collected Works of St. John of the Cross:* ICS Publications, Washington, DC, 92.

Putting it All Together: *Lectio Divina*

> I would like in particular to recall and recommend the ancient tradition of *Lectio divina:* the diligent reading of Sacred Scripture accompanied by prayer brings about that intimate dialogue in which the person reading hears God who is speaking, and in praying, responds to him with trusting openness of heart (cf. *Dei Verbum,* 25). If it is effectively promoted, this practice will bring to the Church—I am convinced of it—a new spiritual springtime.
>
> —Pope Benedict XVI[4]

One of the best ways to "talk," "listen," and "be with" God in a single sitting is the time-honored method of praying with Scripture called *lectio divina* (Latin for "divine reading"). Four "Rs" give a simple description of how to do it.

First, **prepare.** Begin with the Sign of the Cross. Take a moment to be quiet and still. Ask the Holy Spirit to guide your time.

1. **Read** the Scripture selection slowly and attentively. Note any word, phrase, or image that catches your attention. It's helpful to read the passage more than once, and/or out loud.

2. **Reflect.** Think about the meaning of whatever caught your attention. The Holy Spirit drew you to it for a reason. What line of thought do you pursue in response? Notice any questions

---

[4] Address to Participants in the International Congress Organized to Commemorate the 40th Anniversary of the Dogmatic Constitution on Divine Revelation *[Dei Verbum]*, September 16, 2005. Accessed at www.vatican.va, https://w2.vatican.va/content/benedict-xvi/en/speeches/2005/september/documents/hf_ben-xvi_spe_20050916_40-dei-verbum.html.

that arise or any emotions you experience. Return to the text as often as you wish.

3. **Respond.** Talk to God about the passage, your thoughts, or anything else on your heart. Thank him for the blessings you received. Ask him for your own needs, and the needs of others. Note any changes or actions you want to make. If the Holy Spirit leads you to any resolution or application in your life, writing it down will help you remember. Ask God to help you to live it out.

4. **Rest**. Rest a few minutes in silence with the Lord. "Be still, and know that I am God" (Psalm 46:10).

Recommended Scripture Passages for *Lectio Divina*

Choose passages that are relatively short. The goal is not to cover a lot of material but to listen "with the ear of our heart," as St. Benedict instructed his monks in his *Rule*.

- Read the Gospel passage of the day for the Mass, found online at bible.usccb.org.

- Slowly work through a Gospel or an epistle, such as Ephesians, Philippians, James, or 1 John.

- Read the psalms.

- Use a Bible app or search online to find reading plans or Scripture passages on topics relevant to your life, such as gratitude, fear, or courage. We're often most attuned to hearing God on topics very important to us personally.

- Many mobile apps will guide you through fifteen minutes of prayer for your 1% time slot. One we especially love is called "Pray as You Go." It uses one of the daily Mass readings from the Scriptures to lead you through a contemplative time.

We only devote periods of quiet time to the things or the people whom we love; and here we are speaking of the God whom we love, a God who wishes to speak to us.
—Pope Francis[5]

My secret is simple: I pray.
—St. Teresa of Calcutta[6]

---

[5] *The Joy of the Gospel*, 146.
[6] *The Power of Prayer* (New York: MJF Books, 1998), 3, 7–8, quoted in *United States Catholic Catechism for Adults* (Washington, DC: United States Conference of Catholic Bishops, 2006), 479.

Appendix

If it has been a long time since you last went to Confession—or if you've never been—you may be hesitant and unsure. Don't let these very common feelings get in your way. Reconciling with God and the Church always brings great joy. Take the plunge—you will be glad you did!

If it will help to alleviate your fears, familiarize yourself with the step-by-step description of the process below. Most priests are happy to help anyone willing to take the risk. If you forget anything, the priest will remind you. So don't worry about committing every step and word to memory. Remember, Jesus isn't giving you a test; he just wants you to experience the grace of his mercy!

Catholics believe that the priest acts *in persona Christi,* "in the person of Christ." The beauty of the sacraments is that they touch us both physically and spiritually. On the physical level in Confession, we hear the words of absolution through the person of the priest. On the spiritual level, we know that it is Christ assuring us that he has truly forgiven us. We are made clean!

You usually have the option of going to Confession anonymously—in a confessional booth or in a room with a screen—or face-to-face with the priest. Whatever your preference will be fine with the priest.

Steps in the Sacrament of Reconciliation:

1. Prepare to receive the sacrament by praying and examining your conscience. If you need help, you can

find many different lists of questions online that will help you examine your conscience.

2. Once you're with the priest, begin by making the Sign of the Cross while greeting the priest with these words: "Bless me, Father, for I have sinned." Then tell him how long it has been since your last confession. If it's your first confession, tell him so.

3. Confess your sins to the priest to the best of your recollection. If you are unsure about anything, ask him to help you. Place your trust in God, who is a merciful and loving Father. When you are finished, indicate this by saying, "I am sorry for these and all of my sins."

4. The priest will assign you a penance, such as a prayer, a Scripture reading, or a work of mercy, service, or sacrifice.

5. Express sorrow for your sins by saying an Act of Contrition, such as the one below. Or you may pray in your own words if desired.

   Act of Contrition
   My God, I am sorry for my sins with all my heart. In choosing to do wrong, and failing to do good, I have sinned against you whom I should love above all things. I firmly intend, with your help, to do penance, to sin no more, and to avoid whatever leads me to sin. Our Savior Jesus Christ suffered and died for us. In his name, my God, have mercy.

6. The priest, acting again in the person of Christ, will absolve you of your sins with prayerful words, ending with, "I absolve you

from your sins in the name of the Father, and of the Son, and of the Holy Spirit." You respond by making the Sign of the Cross and saying, "Amen."

7. The priest may offer some proclamation of praise.

8. The priest will dismiss you, often with the words "Your sins are forgiven. Go in peace."

9. Be sure to complete your assigned penance as soon as possible.

Appendices for Facilitators

D The Role of a Facilitator

E A Guide for Each Session of *Amazed and Afraid*

F Leading Prayer and "Encountering Christ This Week"

Appendix

Perhaps no skill is more important to the success of a small group than the ability to facilitate a discussion lovingly. It is God's Holy Spirit working through our personal spiritual journey, not necessarily our theological knowledge, that makes this possible.

The following guidelines can help facilitators avoid some of the common pitfalls of small group discussion. The goal is to open the door for the Spirit to take the lead and guide your every response because you are attuned to his movements.

Pray daily and before your small group meeting. This is the only way you can learn to sense the Spirit's gentle promptings when they come!

You Are a Facilitator, Not a Teacher

As a facilitator, it can be extremely tempting to answer every question. You may have excellent answers and be excited about sharing them with your brothers and sisters in Christ. However, a more Socratic method, by which you attempt to draw answers from participants, is much more fruitful for everyone else and for you as well.

Get in the habit of reflecting participants' questions or comments to the whole group before offering your own input. It is not necessary for you as a facilitator to enter immediately into the discussion or to offer a magisterial answer. When others have sufficiently addressed an issue, try to exercise restraint in your comments. Simply affirm what has been said; then thank them and move on.

If you don't know the answer to a question, have a participant look it up in the *Catechism of the Catholic Church* and read it aloud to the group. If you cannot find an answer, ask someone to research the question for the next session. Never feel embarrassed to say, "I don't know." Simply acknowledge the quality of the question and offer to follow up with that person after you have done some digging. Remember, you are a facilitator, not a teacher.

Affirm and Encourage
We are more likely to repeat a behavior when it is openly encouraged. If you want more active participation and sharing, give positive affirmation to the responses of the group members. This is especially important if people are sharing from their hearts. A simple "Thank you for sharing that" can go a long way in encouraging further discussion in your small group.

If someone has offered a theologically questionable response, don't be nervous or combative. Wait until others have offered their input. It is very likely that someone will proffer a more helpful response, which you can affirm by saying something such as "That is the Christian perspective on that topic. Thank you."

If no acceptable response is given and you know the answer, exercise great care and respect in your comments so as not to appear smug or self-righteous. You might begin with something such as "Those are all interesting perspectives. What the Church has said about this is . . . "

Avoid Unhelpful Tangents
Nothing can derail a Spirit-filled discussion more quickly than digressing on unnecessary tangents. Try to keep the session on track. If conversation strays from the topic, ask yourself, "Is this a

Spirit-guided tangent?" Ask the Holy Spirit too! If not, bring the group back by asking a question that steers conversation to the Scripture passage or to a question you have been discussing. You may even suggest kindly, "Have we gotten a little off topic?" Most participants will respond positively and get back on track through your sensitive leading.

That being said, some tangents may be worth pursuing if you sense a movement of the Spirit. It may be exactly where God wants to steer the discussion. You will find that taking risks can yield some beautiful results.

Don't Fear the Silence

Be okay with silence. Most people need a moment or two to come up with a response to a question. People naturally require some time to formulate their thoughts and put them into words. Some may need a few moments just to gather the courage to speak at all.

Regardless of the reason, don't be afraid of a brief moment of silence after asking a question. Let everyone in the group know early on that silence is an integral part of normal small group discussion. They needn't be anxious or uncomfortable when it happens. God works in silence!

This applies to times of prayer as well. If no one shares or prays after a sufficient amount of time, just move on gracefully.

The Power of Hospitality

A little hospitality can go far in creating community. Everyone likes to feel cared for. This is especially true in a small group whose purpose it is to connect to Jesus Christ, a model for care, support, and compassion.

Make a point to greet people personally when they first arrive. Ask them how their day has been going. Take some time to invest in the lives of your small group participants. Pay particular attention to newcomers. Work at remembering each person's name. Help everyone feel comfortable and at home. Allow your small group to be an environment in which authentic relationships take shape and blossom.

Encourage Participation
Help everyone to get involved, especially those who are naturally less vocal or outgoing. To encourage participation initially, always invite various group members to read aloud the selected readings. Down the road, even after the majority of the group feels comfortable sharing, you may still have some quieter members who rarely volunteer a response to a question but would be happy to read.

Meteorology?
Keep an eye on the "Holy Spirit barometer." Is the discussion pleasing to the Holy Spirit? Is this conversation leading participants to a deeper personal connection to Jesus Christ? The intellectual aspects of our faith are certainly important to discuss, but conversation can sometimes degenerate into an unedifying showcase of intellect and ego. Other times discussion becomes an opportunity for gossip, detraction, complaining, or even slander. When this happens, you can almost feel the Holy Spirit leaving the room!

If you are aware that this dynamic has taken over a discussion, take a moment to pray quietly in your heart. Ask the Holy Spirit to help you bring the conversation to a more wholesome topic. This can often be achieved simply by moving to the next question.

Pace

Generally, you want to pace the session to finish in the allotted time, but sometimes this may be impossible without sacrificing quality discussion. If you reach the end of your meeting and find that you have covered only half the material, don't fret! This is often the result of lively Spirit-filled discussion and meaningful theological reflection.

In such a case, you may take time at another meeting to cover the remainder of the material. If you have only a small portion left, you can ask participants to pray through these on their own and come to the following meeting with any questions or insights they may have. Even if you must skip a section to end on time, make sure you leave adequate time for prayer and to review the "Encounter Christ This Week" section. This is vital in helping participants integrate their discoveries from the group into their daily lives.

Genuine Friendships

The best way to show Jesus' love and interest in your small group members is to meet with them for coffee, dessert, or a meal outside of your small group time.

You can begin by suggesting that the whole group get together for ice cream or some other social event at a different time than when your group usually meets. Socializing will allow relationships to develop. It provides the opportunity for different kinds of conversations than small group sessions allow. You will notice an immediate difference in the quality of community in your small group at the next meeting.

After that first group social, try to meet one-on-one with each person in your small group. This allows for more indepth conversation and personal sharing, giving you the chance to know each participant better so that you can love and care for them as Jesus would.

Jesus called the twelve apostles in order that they could "be with him" (Mark 3:14). When people spend time together, eat together, laugh together, cry together, and talk about what matters to them, intense Christian community develops. That is the kind of community Jesus was trying to create, and that must be the kind of community we try to create, because it changes lives. And changed lives change the world!

Joy

Remember that seeking the face of the Lord brings joy! Nothing is more fulfilling, more illuminating, and more beautiful than fostering a deep and enduring relationship with Jesus Christ. Embrace your participants and the entire spiritual journey with a spirit of joyful anticipation of what God wants to accomplish.

> *"These things I have spoken to you, that my joy may be in you, and that your joy may be full." (John 15:11)*

Appendix

God can respond to us personally through the Scriptures, whether or not we know anything about biblical times. God can also speak to us through commonly known information about the social and religious situations in the era when Jesus lived. These notes will help you assist your group to better understand the Scriptures you read each week by providing you with brief summaries of information that may be relevant to your conversation about the passages.

While some of these historical and religious facts are fascinating, always resist any urge to teach rather than facilitate conversation. The EC provides this information in case discussion would benefit from it. Sometimes it will be relevant and helpful in the conversation, sometimes not. When a little information will add clarity and illuminate a discussion, share briefly—ideally in your own words. Then ask how it can deepen an understanding of what was happening and what it means for us today. In other words, give the conversation back to the group as quickly as possible.

Some of these notes pertain to the needs of a group at a particular time. The notes for Week 1 include suggestions on ways to make people feel comfortable, while the notes for Week 6 suggest ideas for encouraging participants to go forward in a deepening life in Christ.

Review the guide for each session as you prepare each week. Jot some notes so that you can summarize the information in your own words should it be relevant to the conversation.

Appendices for Facilitators

"My son, your sins are forgiven."
— Mark 2:5

Week 1
Healing of the Paralytic—Mark 2:1-12

Introductions

Everyone in your small group may not know one another. The first time you meet, you can set people at ease by asking a few conversational questions. Use the ones we have suggested below, or formulate your own.

In choosing questions, it's important that they have no right or wrong answer; choose topics about which no one could feel that their answer is the only right one. Be sure to avoid anything controversial. During this conversation, also ask people to share their names. If yours is a campus group, you may want people to name the residence hall, sorority/fraternity, or neighborhood where they live. Some parish groups ask people to say how many years they've been at the parish.

- Who is the greatest quarterback in the NFL?

- What is your ideal vacation?

Here are some examples of responses that might help you think about what other questions you could ask:

- "I'm Greg. I'm a freshman in _____ (dorm) and a friend of _____. He made me come. I think that Peyton Manning is the greatest quarterback the NFL has ever seen or ever will!"

- "I'm Leslie, mother of three and a parishioner at St. Luke's for the last five years. The best way I could spend a vacation is to have a full-time nanny for a week—*anywhere*."

Scripture Discussion

Again, these facts may or may not be relevant to the conversation. Raise them only if they answer questions or provide direction for a conversation that needs it.

Location: Jesus was from Nazareth, but his early ministry happened in and around Capernaum. Scholars guess that he was at Simon's house because the healing of Peter's mother-in-law happens in these Capernaum chapters. (Simon is later called "Peter" by Jesus, because the Greek word for "rock" is *petra*. Jesus says that Simon will now be called Peter, the rock on which he will build the Church—see Matthew 16:8.)

Themes: While we ask no question about Jesus forgiving the sins of the paralytic, it will probably come up in the conversation about the scribes' response to Jesus. In first-century Judaism, sin and sickness were often associated. The Jews of that time believed that the sins of the parents could be visited on their children. (In John 9:3, in the story of the man born blind, Jesus directly addresses these beliefs: "It was not that this man sinned, or his parents, but that the works of God might be made manifest in him.")[1] This is interesting, but the story is less about Jewish thought on sin and illness and more about Jesus revealing who he is through what he says and does.

Question #2: People may wonder what would be involved with breaking through a house roof. Roofs in that area at that time

[1] *The Anchor Bible: Mark 1-8*, by Joel Marcus (New York: Doubleday, 2000), 221.

were made of wooden beams covered with thatch and mud,[2] easy to dig through but requiring hard physical labor to repair. Many had ladders because of the work a roof required.

If the group doesn't enter imaginatively into the scene, ask questions to help prompt them:

- What would it be like to carry a pallet, "a poor man's bed,"[3] through the streets of a town in the ancient Near East?
- Have you ever had to carry a person a long distance?
- Has anyone ever tried to get close to a stage in a crowd? What was that like?
- How do you think the four men might have hauled the paralytic up to the roof?
- What do you think was involved with making a hole in the roof and lowering the paralytic through it?
- Have you ever tried to hold a rope with a heavy weight and let it out slowly? What happens?

Question #5: If anyone should ask, the scribes were literally "people of letters"—*grammateus* in Greek. The word corresponds roughly to "secretary" in English, and in both languages indicates anything from a person who copies letters or transcribes an author to a high government official. For example, the US has a "Secretary" of State, who no doubt has many administrative assistants who could be described as "secretaries" as well.

---

[2] *The New Jerome Biblical Commentary*, edited by Raymond E Brown, S.S., Joseph A. Fitzmyer, S.J., and Roland E. Murphy, O. Carm. (Englewood Cliffs, NJ: Prentice Hall, 1990), 601.
[3] Marcus, 216.

In the Gospel of Mark, a scribe is a sage or a teacher who interprets the Law. The crowds sometimes compare Jesus' teaching to what the scribes taught because the scribes were the teachers of the Law with whom the people were most familiar.[4]

Question #6: The conversation could go many directions. This quote from the psalms may or may not be relevant:

> Search me, O God, and know my heart!
> Try me and know my thoughts!
> And see if there be any wicked way in me,
> and lead me in the way everlasting!
> (Psalm 139:23-24)

Week 2
The Call of Matthew—Matthew 9:9-13

Location: The call of Matthew happens right after the healing of the paralytic in two of the four Gospels: Mark and Matthew. Matthew is called Levi in the Gospel of Mark. Scholars generally concur that this scene took place in the town of Capernaum.

Question #6: In the four Gospels of the New Testament, the Pharisees often criticize Jesus or inquire why he is doing something. Josephus, the preeminent Jewish historian of this period,

---
[4] Ibid., 523.

describes the Pharisees "as the most accurate interpreters of the law and influential among the common people." Pharisees zealously observed all the Jewish laws, including the oral tradition, which was very extensive.[5]

The Pharisees ask Jesus' disciples why their master eats with tax collectors and sinners, because dining with those who were considered ritually unclean, or touching them, would have made Jesus unclean as well. The Pharisees believed that people who worked with the Romans or any Gentiles or did not observe Jewish ritual purification laws such as washing after contact with certain people or things, and before meals, were "sinners" and posed genuine spiritual danger. They couldn't understand a Jewish teacher (a rabbi) blatantly ignoring the ritual purity laws.

Question #9: For Jews of Jesus' time, the word "sacrifice" almost always referred to a ritual act of worship in which an animal was offered to God. The Old Testament gives many instructions about which animals to sacrifice and how to do it. For more information, see Bible Odyssey,[6] the online version of the *Harper Collins Bible Dictionary*. This is a terrific free resource whenever you need a simple definition on something you don't know in the Scriptures.

---

[5] Ibid., 521–22.
[6] Accessed at https://www.bibleodyssey.org/HarperCollinsBibleDictionary/s/sacrifice.aspx/.

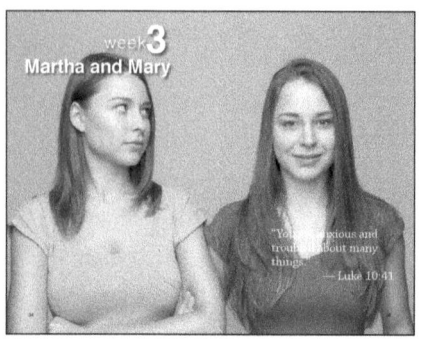

Week 3
Martha and Mary—
Luke 10:38-42

Location: At the end of chapter 9 in Luke's Gospel, Jesus begins traveling from Galilee to Jerusalem to meet his fate. He is on that journey when he visits his friends Mary and Martha, who must have lived in a village somewhere between Galilee and Jerusalem.

Question #1: The translation of verse 40 in the RSVCE is somewhat misleading. In the original Greek, Martha uses the imperative mood for the verb translated "tell," but the subjunctive mood for the words translated as "to help me." The subjunctive indicates something that is wanted, expected, or hoped for but not a given. Martha insists that Jesus talk to Mary ("Tell her"), but she is less insistent about what he should say ("to help me"). *The New Jerusalem Bible* (an approved Catholic translation) translates the Greek into English as "*Please* tell her to help me" (emphasis added). You may want to share this translation if your group makes assumptions about Martha based on the RSVCE translation.

Encountering Christ This Week: Tell people that the following week the group will share about their experiences with these prayer exercises. Encourage them to pray the exercises so that they have something to share.

Appendices for Facilitators

Week 4
Jesus Calls the First Disciples—
Luke 5:1-11

Opening Discussion: The exercises in the last "Encountering Christ This Week" section ask people to pray about their relationship with Jesus: what it has been like and what they want it to be.

If participants don't open up about their prayer and thoughts, ask them if they were able to do the "Encountering Christ" exercises. If most group members say yes, share something from your own prayer to ease the way for another person to speak. Being vulnerable first often helps others share more easily when no one is saying anything. Arrive prepared to describe what these considerations unearthed for you. This will be easier if you take notes each time you pray this week.

If most in the group say they weren't able to do the suggested prayer exercises, then suggest that they pray over them in the coming week so that all can share their experiences and thoughts at the next meeting. In your own words, tell the group that these are important questions of faith that all Christians should ask themselves. Explain in your own words that thinking through these questions is crucial if we want to grow as disciples of Jesus or even for deciding whether we want to follow him at all. Talking about these central matters of the faith will help participants grow in their relationships with one another as well. Close by encouraging group members to take the time they need in the coming week to ask themselves what they really think and believe about Jesus.

If participants did pray through the exercises and you have the discussion this week, don't be afraid to allow periods of silence after you or anyone else shares. The Holy Spirit works in silence!

Location: Gennesaret is another name for the Sea of Galilee. It is the name of an extended plain that adjoins the lake.

Encountering Christ This Week: The exercises this week include encouragement regarding the Sacrament of Reconciliation. If you have your own positive experiences of Confession, share one with the group. No need to discuss details of any particular sin. Focus on the feelings that followed: relief, freedom—whatever you felt. Even Catholics need a lot of encouragement to overcome their fears about this sacrament. One of the best gifts you can give is to share how Jesus has given you "life to the fullest" (cf. John 10:10) through Confession and absolution. Speaking generally about your own experience rather than about any specific sin will model for others how to discuss Reconciliation.

If participants have had distressing experiences of Confession in the past, allow them to share these. Talking about them can bring healing. Don't allow the conversation to wallow in negative stories, however. Recognize that someone has been hurt. When you acknowledge their pain and say you're sorry that this happened to them, you say it for the whole Church. Then move on.

If you know of confessors who are pastorally gifted, share their names and parishes or institutions; it may encourage people who fear the sacrament. So too could reminding the group that everything anyone confesses is under a seal: the priest can never speak of it to anyone.

Share some of your own positive experiences or a general explanation of why you find Confession helpful. Encourage people to try confessors you know who are pastorally gifted.

If you're Catholic and this sacrament isn't already part of your life, we strongly recommend that you seek out Reconciliation before the meeting so that you have something to share. Ask Catholics you know to recommend gifted confessors.

Week 5
Asleep in the Boat—Mark 4:35-41

Location: Once again on the Sea of Galilee, the scene of many of Jesus' miracles.

Question #1: Follow the lead of the Holy Spirit, but if the conversation doesn't flow, ask questions to help participants notice details. For example,

- What time of day was it?
- Would you usually set sail in the evening?
- Who instigates this evening sail and why?
- Do they sail alone?

Amazed and Afraid: Discover the Power of Jesus

Week 6
The Way to the Father—John 14:1-11

Opening Discussion: As you discuss the "Encountering Christ" exercise, take time to draw attention to any evidence you see in participants' responses that God has helped them grow or change during the six weeks of this group. Praise God for the changes that their prayer experiences reveal. If you still have time afterward, ask the opening discussion question; if not, skip it.

Scripture: Before someone reads the Scripture passage, provide context for it. (Relate it to the opening discussion question if you asked it.) In your own words, say something such as this:

> Today/tonight we will read part of what Jesus said to his closest followers the night he was arrested and tried—the events leading up to his execution. His words have weight because they're the things Jesus wanted his disciples to know right before he left them. Let's think about the reading in light of those circumstances.
>
> It would take too much time to read about all of the events of this night. It could be helpful to know, however, that before this teaching, Jesus predicted both that he would be betrayed by Judas and denied three times by Peter.

Questions #1 and #3: If participants don't respond, draw out the details by asking them questions such as

11. Why do you think he teaches _____ to them at this time?
12. What does he mean by _____?
13. How do you think the disciples felt when he said that?

Question #5: This topic may have come up from your discussions of questions 1–4. If so, skip to #6.

Encountering Christ This Week: Mention that even though group members have reached the end of this small group series, it's not the end of their relationship with God in Christ! For some, it might be just the beginning. Encourage people to keep praying at least fifteen minutes a day with Scripture so that their relationship with Jesus can continue to grow. Assure them that from this small chunk of time, God can give them the love and graces he wants all his beloved children to have.

Conclusion: Ask your group whether they want to continue meeting. (That would be a gift from God and a tribute to your ability to facilitate well and create a loving community.) The Evangelical Catholic offers other small group guides that you could use for discussion (see our store at evangelicalcatholic.org). Other organizations and authors publish small group guides as well.

Your group doesn't need a guide, however. You could study the Sunday Mass readings or read through a book of the Bible together and develop your own questions. If you decide to explore the Bible, you can find many books and online resources on how to ask questions of the text that lead to fruitful discussion. The United States Conference of Catholic Bishops has excellent principles and resources for reading the Bible on its website (see usccb.org/bible/understanding-the-bible/index.cfm).

Whether or not you continue meeting, thank the members of your group for the commitment they made and the time they gave. It's a great honor to walk with people on their spiritual journeys. Share that sentiment if you are moved to do so.

Try to have a more celebratory atmosphere at this last session by providing a dessert or other treat during the social time. You could ask members to bring something to share.

Appendix

Opening Prayer

We have provided a guided opening prayer for each session because it can help people who are completely new to small groups and shared extemporaneous prayer feel more at ease. If everyone or most people present are already comfortable speaking to God in their own words aloud in a group, you won't need these prayers at all. It's always better to talk to God from our hearts in a small group. It contributes to the intimacy of the group and also builds individual intimacy with God.

Since some people have never witnessed spontaneous prayer, it's part of your role to model it. Prayers from the heart spoken aloud demonstrate how to talk to God honestly and openly. Seeing someone pray this way expands a person's understanding of who God is and the relationship he or she can have with Jesus Christ.

You can grow in extemporaneous prayer by praying aloud directly to Jesus during your personal prayer time and as you prepare for the group. This will help "prime the pump," so to speak.

Even if you enjoy praying aloud spontaneously, your goal as a facilitator is to provide opportunities for everyone to grow spiritually. People who pray aloud with others grow in leaps and bounds—we've seen it! After the first meeting, tell the group that you will allow time at the end of your extemporaneous prayer for others to voice prayers. As soon as the group appears to have grown into this, invite other people to open the group with prayer instead of leading it yourself or using the prayer provided.

If you don't do it in the first meeting, in the second week, pray the opening prayer in your own words. Here are some simple parts to include:

1. Praise God! Say what a great and wonderful God our Father is. Borrow language from the psalms of praise if you don't have your own. Just search online for "praise psalms."

2. Thank God! Thank the Lord for the gift of gathering together. Thank him for giving each person present the desire to sacrifice their time to attend the group. Thank him for the blessing of your parish or campus community.

3. Ask God for your needs. Ask God to bless your time together and to make it fruitful for all present as well as for his kingdom. Ask Jesus to be with you, who are two or three gathered in his name. Ask the Holy Spirit to open hearts, illuminate minds, and deepen each person's experience through the Scripture passages you'll read and discuss. Ask the Holy Spirit to guide the discussion so that you can all grow from it.

4. Close by invoking Jesus: "We pray this through Christ our Lord" or "We pray this in Jesus' name."

5. End with the Sign of the Cross.

Some essentials for extemporaneous prayer:

- Speak in the first-person plural "we." For example, "Holy Spirit, we ask you to open our hearts . . . " It's fine to add a line asking the Holy Spirit to help you facilitate the discussion as he wills, or something else to that effect, but most of the prayer should be for the whole group.

- Model speaking directly to Jesus our Lord. This may sound obvious, but among Catholic laypeople, it isn't frequently practiced or modeled. This is a very evangelical thing to do in the sense that it witnesses to the gospel. Not only does it show how much we believe that the Lord loves us, but it also demonstrates our confidence that Jesus himself is listening to us! As we say our Lord's name, we remind ourselves, as well as those who hear us, that we aren't just talking to ourselves. This builds up faith.

You and anyone unaccustomed to hearing someone pray to Jesus directly may feel a bit uncomfortable at first. But group members will quickly become more at ease as they hear these prayers repeatedly and experience more intimacy with Jesus. Bear in mind always that many graces come from praying "the name which is above every name" (Philippians 2:9).

If you've never publicly prayed to Jesus, you may feel childish at first, but pray for the humility of a child. After all, Jesus did say that we needed to become like children (Matthew 18:3)! The more we pray directly to Jesus in our personal prayer, the less awkward it will feel when we pray to him publicly.

- Model great faith and trust that the Lord hears your prayer and will answer it. It's terrific just to say in prayer, "Jesus, we trust you!"

- You can always close extemporaneous prayer by inviting the whole group to join in a prayer of the Church, such as the Glory Be, the Our Father, or the Hail Mary. This will bring all into the prayer if previously, just one person was praying aloud extemporaneously.

Closing Prayer

For the closing prayer, we recommend that you always include extemporaneous prayer, even if you also use the prayer provided. No written prayer can address the thoughts, concerns, feelings, and inspirations that come up during the discussion.

If some group members already feel comfortable praying aloud in their own words, invite the group to join in the closing prayer right away. If not, wait a week or two. Once you feel that the group has the familiarity to prevent this from being too awkward, invite them to participate. You could tell the group that you will begin the closing prayer and then allow for a time of silence so that they can also pray aloud. Make sure they know that you will close the group's prayer by leading them into an Our Father after everyone is done praying spontaneously. This structure helps people feel that the time is contained and not completely lacking in structure. That helps free them to pray aloud.

Below are some possible ways to introduce your group to oral extemporaneous prayer. Don't read these suggestions verbatim—put them into your own words. It's not conducive to helping people become comfortable praying aloud spontaneously if you are reading out of a book!

"The closing prayer is a great time to take the reflections we've shared, bring them to God, and ask him to help us make any inspirations a reality in our lives. God doesn't care about how well-spoken or articulate we are when we pray, so we shouldn't either! We don't judge each other's prayers. Let's just pray from our hearts, knowing that God hears and cares about what we say, not how perfectly we say it. When we pray something aloud, we know that the Holy Spirit is mightily at work within us because it's the Spirit who gives us the courage to speak."

"Tonight for the closing prayer, let's first each voice our needs to one another; then we will take turns putting our right hand on the shoulder of the person to the right of us and praying for that person. After we each express our prayer needs, I will start by praying for Karen on my right. That means that I need to listen carefully when she tells us what she needs prayer for. We may not remember everyone's needs, so be sure to listen well to the person on your right. I'll voice my prayer needs first; then we'll go around the circle to the right. Then I will begin with the Sign of the Cross and pray for _____ (name of person to the right) with my hand on his of her shoulder. Okay? Does anyone have any questions?"

Encountering Christ This Week

These weekly prayer and reflection exercises allow Jesus to enter more fully into the hearts of you and your small group members. If we don't give God the time that allows him to work in us, we experience far less fruit from our small group discussions. Prayer and reflection water the seeds that have been planted during the small group so they can take root. Without the "water" of prayer and reflection, the sun will scorch the seed, and it will shrivel up and die, "since it had no root" (Mark 4:6). Encountering Christ during the week on our own makes it possible for us to be "rooted in Christ" (cf. Colossians 2:7) and to drink deeply of the "living water" (John 4:10) that he longs to pour into our souls.

Please review the "Encountering Christ This Week" section in advance so that you're familiar with it, and then together as a group during each meeting. Reviewing it together will show everyone that it is an important part of the small group. Ask for feedback each week about how these prayer and reflection exercises are going. Don't spend too long on this topic, however, especially in the early weeks while members are still becoming comfortable together and growing more accustomed to praying on their own. Asking about their experience with the recommended prayer, sacrament, or spiritual exercise will help you know who is hungry for spiritual growth and who might need more encouragement. The witness of participants' stories from their times of prayer can ignite the interest of others who are less motivated to pray.

Small Group Discussion Guides from the Evangelical Catholic

Amazed and Afraid: Discover the Power of Jesus

Small Group Discussion Guides

When people meet the real Jesus in Scripture, lives change, hearts heal, and the grace and power of our Baptism is unleashed to make us "ambassadors for Christ" (2 Corinthians 5:20). Using these guides, well-formed and trained leaders who've learned to facilitate dynamic Scripture discussions can be instruments of the Holy Spirit revealing the person of Jesus. Order books at evangelicalcatholic.org.

Encounter Series

The Evangelical Catholic's Encounter Series of books and resources are designed to connect people with Jesus through prayer and Scripture. They are approachable for anyone desiring a deeper experience of Jesus.

Believe: Meeting Jesus in the Scriptures

The six sessions in *Believe: Meeting Jesus in the Scriptures* focus on episodes when Jesus changed people's lives. Get to know Jesus as he heals a blind man, mourns the death of a friend, and has compassion on the people he meets. The questions that follow spark discussion and allow participants to consider how the story applies to their own lives.

Small Group Discussion Guides from the Evangelical Catholic

Amazed and Afraid: Discover the Power of Jesus

Dive into the Gospels and begin a regular pattern of prayer. Each of the six sessions in *Amazed and Afraid: Discover the Power of Jesus* features a scene about Jesus and his disciples, followed by a series of questions to help participants reflect more deeply on their relationship with God.

Signs and Wonders: Encountering Jesus of Nazareth

The Gospels reveal what Jesus cared about, how he treated people, and what he thought was most important in life. The six sessions of *Signs and Wonders: Encountering Jesus of Nazareth* include some of the most dramatic Gospel episodes: the wedding at Cana, Jesus walking on water, and raising a little girl who had died. Discussion questions help participants ponder Jesus' power in their own lives.

Establish Series

The Evangelical Catholic's Establish Series of books and resources help participants build a solid foundation of discipleship in their lives. They are perfect for anyone ready to grow their commitment to following Jesus.

The Way: Becoming a Disciple of Jesus

Catholic disciples mature to the extent that they allow the ways of Jesus to become ever more their own. In *The Way: Becoming a Disciple of Jesus,* partipants reflect on the call to know God as friend, savior, and source of all life through Jesus Christ. Over twelve sessions, participants grow in the heart and habits of discipleship, including prayer, Scripture, the sacramental life, community, and evangelization. *The Way* includes readings from Scripture and Tradition, discussion questions, prompts for take-home prayer and action steps, and appendices for both participants and facilitators.

Small Group Discussion Guides from the Evangelical Catholic

Transformed: The Gift and Challenge of the Eucharist

The Eucharist is both an indescribable gift and a profound challenge. What effect does this sacred mystery have on those who receive it? In a word, *transformation*. As the bread and wine are truly transformed into the Body and Blood of Jesus, those who receive this heavenly meal with open hearts are continually transformed into people who love like Jesus—and loving like Jesus transforms the world.

In this six-week Catholic discussion guide for small groups, participants read and discuss key selections from Scripture, saints, and Church teaching around the transformational power and promise of the Eucharist.

With Jesus to the Cross: Lenten Guides on the Sunday Mass Readings

On the night before he died, Jesus made this promise to his disciples: "If you continue in my word, you are truly my disciples, and you will know the truth, and the truth will make you free" (John 8:31-32). *With Jesus to the Cross* makes it easy for small groups or individuals to dive into the Lenten Sunday Mass readings with thought-provoking questions. Available for liturgical years A, B, and C.

About the Evangelical Catholic

The Evangelical Catholic (EC) is a Catholic non-profit consulting ministry based in Madison, Wisconsin. The Evangelical Catholic delights to partner with Catholic ministry leaders to equip everyday Catholics to live out the great commission.

In 1997, Tim and Sandy Cruse started a small group of Catholics in their home. This group experienced Jesus powerfully through intimate friendship, rich Scripture discussions, and shared sacramental experiences. After one year, the people from this group went out to form their own small groups with friends, co-workers, neighbors, and family that they hoped would come to experience Jesus in the same way. With immense joy, these leaders experienced that they could make disciples by the power of the Holy Spirit given to them in their Baptism.

Filled with the Holy Spirit, these leaders sparked a movement of evangelization that extended to reach more and more people. As word spread about this expanding movement of evangelization, the EC helped other ministries launch lay people into mission by leading training events, writing small group guides, and traveling to ministries across the United States.

Today, the Evangelical Catholic works with hundreds of parishes, campus ministries, and military chaplaincies worldwide. Our prayer is that through the grace of the Holy Spirit, we can help make the Church's mission of evangelization accessible, natural, and fruitful for every Catholic, and that many lives will be healed and transformed by knowing Jesus within the Church.

Learn more at evangelicalcatholic.org.

www.ingramcontent.com/pod-product-compliance
Lightning Source LLC
Chambersburg PA
CBHW042115100526
44587CB00025B/4067